Marine Aquarium Keeping

Marine Aquarium Keeping

Second Edition

STEPHEN SPOTTE, Ph.D.
Marine Sciences Institute
The University of Connecticut
Noank, Connecticut

John Wiley & Sons, Inc.
NEW YORK / CHICHESTER / BRISBANE / TORONTO / SINGAPORE

This text is printed on acid-free paper.

Library of Congress Cataloging in Publication Data:

Spotte, Stephen
Marine aquarium keeping / Stephen Spotte. — 2nd ed.
p. cm.
Includes bibliographical references (p.) and index.
ISBN 0-471-59489-X (paper : acid-free paper)
1. Marine aquariums. I. Title.
SD457.1.S66 1993
639.3'42—dc20 92–46459

Printed in the United States of America

10 9 8 7 6 5 4 3 2 1

Contents

Preface

This is a no-frills, no-nonsense book about marine aquarium keeping written for beginners. In the following pages I explain how to achieve success on a modest budget. The approach taken emphasizes the needs of living marine animals—principally fishes—while relegating technology to its proper background role. I ask the reader to settle back and resist the siren song of gadgetry. It has yet to be demonstrated that the survival of marine organisms in aquariums is enhanced measurably by the use of complex and expensive equipment. Biology, not gadgetry, is the platform of success.

"Living reef" aquariums, which are devoted mainly to *invertebrates* (animals without backbones) and ornamental algae, are not discussed. The marine aquarium referred to in this book is the *conventional marine aquarium*, a streamlined apparatus that relies on a subgravel filter powered by air for its life-support function. Additional equipment (power filters, ozone generators, foam fractionators) is not necessary and greatly increases the initial cost. Patience, on the other hand, costs nothing. Spend time, not dollars, on your hobby. Learn correct maintenance procedures, devise a rigorous program of disease prevention, and develop good feeding practices. These and other skills are acquired through knowledge and insight, not by the application of technology.

The approach offered here is embodied in three words: look, see, understand. *Look* at your aquarium regularly and often. *See* that the life it holds consists not of mechanistic ornaments but living, breathing inhabitants. *Understand* when what you have looked at and seen deviates from the normal and requires attention. If this advice is followed, your aquarium will thrive.

Portions of the text caution beginning aquarists not to acquire certain animals because their likelihood of surviving is poor. The color plates include representatives of these in addition to others that survive well in captivity. Knowing which groups of animals to embrace and avoid are equally important. In the end, the best advice anyone can offer for selecting animals is to use good judgment.

Each chapter is prefaced by a synopsis, or summary. To benefit completely from the information offered, I recommend that you read the synopsis both before and after reading the text. Important concepts, having once been stated, occasionally reappear in later chapters. Such redundancies are intentional, not an editorial oversight, and represent an attempt to develop a web of continuity. Ideas repeated in a different context help foster understanding. Finally, I neither endorse nor denigrate any of the numerous commercial products depicted in the book. I have included them as examples of what aquarists might find to serve their needs.

STEPHEN SPOTTE

Noank, Connecticut
March 1993

Acknowledgments

Several people helped with preparation of the manuscript. Colleagues Gary Adams and Patricia M. Bubucis assisted with ideas and advice. Gary Adams, Thomas A. Frakes, Lucia S. Spotte, and an anonymous editor read the text and offered many valuable suggestions. Because I occasionally rejected their advice, any incorrect statements are fully my responsibility, and the opinions expressed are mine alone. Credits are provided with tabular and illustrative material reprinted or adapted from other sources. The absence of a credit indicates that the work is my own. John E. Randall graciously supplied color transparencies of fish species lacking in my collection, and his contributions are credited in the color plates. Joseph T. O'Neill prepared the graphics, and James T. Spencer processed and printed the black and white film used in the halftones and made the color-to-halftone conversions. The manufacturers contacted permitted the use of illustrative material. My wife, Lucia, let me trash the kitchen during trials to devise improved gelatin-based fish foods, and she served as photographer's assistant. All these contributions are gratefully acknowledged.

CHAPTER

1 The Aquariums

Synopsis *Place the exhibit aquarium—the unit to be decorated and maintained permanently—where your family congregates, not in an isolated room. The room lights should be wired to a rheostat (also called a dimmer switch) so they can be dimmed gradually at the end of the day. Aquarium animals become stressed if the lights are turned off or on suddenly. When selecting a location, leave space for pedestrian traffic and for you to work. Be sure the floor can support the weight of a full aquarium and stand. Also consider the ambient room light, placement of heating and air conditioning ducts, effect of water spills on floors, clearance for swinging doors, and other factors. Only all-glass aquariums are acceptable. The exhibit aquarium should hold at least 30 gal; a 50-gal unit is preferable. Also needed are a quarantine aquarium (20 gal) and a treatment aquarium (10 gal). Level all aquariums before filling them.*

The contents of this, the opening chapter, will seem strange to someone who has never kept a home aquarium. Such terms as *filter plate* and *biological filtration* will soon become familiar. Many people learn faster through participation; consequently, the book has been organized in a sequential format. Practical advice is supplemented throughout with the necessary theoretical information. Important text statements are set in italics for emphasis.

Read Chapters 1 through 8 and consult Table 1 before buying anything. Your initial objective is to learn how a marine aquarium operates. What matters now is attention to detail. Understanding will come with further reading and experience. *Look* at the equipment you need to get started. *See* how it functions. Procedures outlined in the first eight chapters recommend that a new ma-

TABLE 1 Summary of equipment and supplies needed to set up and maintain exhibit, quarantine, and treatment aquariums.

Equipment and Supplies	Comments
All-glass aquariums (3)	Exhibit (30+ gal), quarantine (20 gal), treatment (10 gal)
Plastic aquarium covers (3)	All aquariums
Reflector with lamps (2)	Optional; necessary for exhibit and quarantine aquariums only if seaweeds are maintained; use cool white or daylight fluorescent lamps, or mix them
Aquarium stand (1)	Exhibit aquarium
Sturdy tables (stands optional)	Quarantine and treatment aquariums
Air compressors, vibrator style (4)	1 large (exhibit aquarium); 5 small (quarantine and treatment aquariums, live food container, 2 plastic corner filters)
Airline tubing	10 feet
Battery-powered aerators (4)	For power failures; two needed for exhibit aquarium
Gang valves and air diffusers	Number optional
Stainless steel washers	For weighting air diffusers; number optional (5/16-inch)
Subgravel filters with airlift pumps	Exhibit, quarantine aquariums
Immersion heaters	All aquariums (2 to 4 watts per gallon of aquarium water)
Carbonate mineral gravel	Exhibit, quarantine aquariums; enough to cover the filter plate to a depth of 2 inches
Plastic jerry cans (number optional)	For collecting seawater (3 to 6 gal each); sufficient total volume to fill the exhibit and quarantine aquariums and administer a 25% water change to the exhibit aquarium
Seawater or artificial sea salts	To fill the exhibit and quarantine aquariums, plus enough to administer a 25% water change to the exhibit aquarium
Artificial seawater mixing container	30+ gal, or sufficient volume to administer a 25% water change to the exhibit aquarium
Commercial dechlorinating agent	Enough to treat the tap water used to dissolve the artificial sea salts
Plastic corner filters (2)	Exhibit, quarantine aquariums
Quilt batting and activated carbon	For plastic corner filters
Aquarium decorations	Exhibit aquarium
Small plastic flower pots (3+)	Quarantine aquarium; of sufficient size for fishes to hide
Seawater test kits	Ammonia, nitrite, nitrate, alkalinity, pH
Hydrometer	For determining specific gravity
Thermometers (3)	Permanently immersed in each aquarium
Notebook	For recording water chemistry data, treatments, dates of animal acquisitions, and so forth
Siphon hoses (3)	3/4-inch clear plastic, one 3-foot length for each aquarium
Calibrated plastic buckets (3+)	3–5 gal, preferably in different colors (one for each aquarium)
Plastic scrub pads (3)	One for each aquarium
Nets (3)	6-inch, fine mesh; one for each aquarium
Nets (2)	4-inch, coarse mesh; for adult brine shrimp
Brine shrimp net or sieve	Sized for brine shrimp nauplii
Heavy plastic freezer bags	For capturing and moving fishes

rine aquarium be placed in full operation, *but without animals and plants* for a minimum of 3 weeks, which is plenty of time to finish reading this book and gain whatever insight it contains.

LOCATING THE AQUARIUM

Aquariums can be placed in any convenient location, but centers of activity are best. A marine aquarium is an object of enjoyment, so place it where everyone will benefit. The kitchen, living room, or den might be suitable (Figure 1). With time, the animals will adjust to your routine movements, and many of the fishes[1] will show noticeable interest in activities around them. Most important, place the aquarium in a room that *you* occupy part of each day, because every moment spent observing will improve your skills as an aquarist.

Avoid locations that are too dark, too bright, close to air conditioning and heating ducts, or in the path of swinging doors. Carpeting and finished hardwood floors seldom survive saltwater

Figure 1 *A marine aquarium is an object of enjoyment. Place it in a center of activity where everyone will benefit. This one has been set up in the the kitchen.*

[1]According to the American Fisheries Society, a *fish* is one or more individuals of the same species. *Fishes* refers to two or more individuals of different species. To state that "three angel*fish* swam past" implies that they all belonged to the same species. However, if one individual was a different species, the phrase should be restated as "three angel*fishes* swam past."

spills for very long. A solid, level floor finished in linoleum or plastic tile is best. Never place a marine aquarium in front of a window. Direct sunlight can cause dangerous temperature fluctuations and unwanted algal growth (see Chapter 14). *The room lights should be wired to a rheostat (also called a dimmer switch) so they can be dimmed gradually at the end of the day. Aquarium animals become stressed if the lights are turned off or on suddenly.*

A full aquarium complete with its stand places considerable strain on a floor. Keep this in mind when choosing a location. Water weighs approximately 7.5 lb/gal.[2] A fully equipped 50-gal aquarium weighs more than 450 lb. Allow 6 inches between the aquarium and the wall for airline tubing and electrical cords and for cleaning the outside back glass. The outside glass surfaces of a marine aquarium become smudged or encrusted with salt and require occasional cleaning.

Consider all these factors and then measure the location selected. Leave enough room for pedestrian traffic (aquariums fare poorly when bumped and banged) and for performing partial water changes and other routine maintenance. Decide how large an aquarium you intend to maintain and visit the dealer.[3] Take along the tape measure and the measurements just made.

CHOOSING THE AQUARIUMS

A modern all-glass aquarium consists of five pieces of glass held together with silicone sealant. The top is trimmed in hard plastic to hold the cover and protect the edges from chipping. Similar trim around the bottom protects against chipping and abrasion from the aquarium stand. Older-style aquariums with metal frames are unsuitable because the frame eventually rusts, ugly brown spots form on its surfaces, and leaks develop.

Aquariums are manufactured in several sizes and two basic rectangular shapes, *high* and *low*. As these names suggest, high models are taller, but not so long as low models of equal volume (Figure 2). Either shape is adequate, but low models offer slightly more room to hold decorations that provide shelter spaces for fishes and *invertebrates* (shrimps, sea anemones, and other animals without backbones). Adequate shelter spaces are important for the survival of captive marine animals (see Chapters 9 and 13). Given a choice, low models are preferable.

At the dealer's store, measure a representative aquarium with its stand to be sure it fits the allocated space. This unit—the one

[2]The symbol for pounds is lb; gal is the symbol for U.S. gallons.

[3]A *dealer* is a proprietor of a retail pet store or tropical fish store.

(a)

(b)

Figure 2 *All-glass aquariums are available in high and low models.* (a) *High model.* (b) *Low model. Low models are preferable.* Source: S. Spotte, *Marine Aquarium Keeping: The Science, Animals, and Art,* John Wiley & Sons, Inc., © 1973, reprinted with permission.

you intend to decorate and maintain permanently—is the *exhibit aquarium.* The minimum recommended size is 30 gal, but a unit holding at least 50 gal is superior from the standpoint of providing an optimal environment. You also need a 20-gal aquarium in which to quarantine new animals and plants *(quarantine aquarium)* and a 10-gal one for treating diseased fishes *(treatment aquarium).*

All three aquariums should have standard covers manufactured in plastic; in other words, the covers must be noncorroding and suitable for saltwater environments. The front inside edge of the hinged lid (the part you raise to feed the animals) should have an inside lip (Figure 3). This allows water that condenses on the underside of the cover to drip back into the aquarium instead of leaking out and leaving salt deposits.

SUPPORTING THE AQUARIUMS

Aquariums can be supported on sturdy tables or commercial aquarium stands. The exhibit aquarium needs a stand; tables are adequate for the quarantine and treatment aquariums. Buy the three aquariums and at least one stand, take them home, and set them in place. Be sure the stand and tables are level before setting aquariums on them. If necessary, shim the legs with wooden wedges and then use a carpenter's level to make a final check. Do not trust your eye. *An unbalanced aquarium is a potential accident*. Be certain once again that the floor can support the final weight.

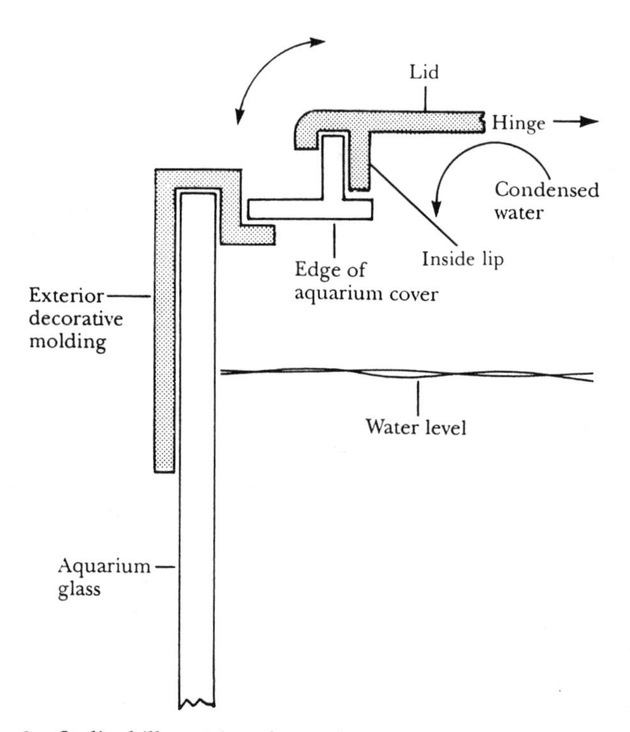

Figure 3 *Stylized illustration of part of a properly designed aquarium cover. The hinged part (the section that is raised to feed the animals) should have an inside lip. This allows water that condenses on the underside of the cover to drain back into the aquarium instead of collecting on the outside.*

C H A P T E R

2 The Air

Synopsis *Marine animals and plants are aerobic, requiring oxygen to survive. During respiration, animals and plants remove oxygen and produce carbon dioxide. Oxygen diffuses into aquarium water from the air, where the concentration is greater. Diffusion is augmented by stirring the surface, which brings oxygen-depleted water into contact with the air and drives excess carbon dioxide out of the aquarium. Stirring is best achieved by aeration, the physical process of bubbling air into water. Aeration enhances gas transfer, the process by which gases (including oxygen) inside air bubbles and at the surface are transferred to the water. Small bubbles transfer gases more effectively than large ones because they have a greater surface-area-to-volume ratio. Purchase a good air compressor of large capacity for the exhibit aquarium. Also purchase five smaller units, one for the live food container and one each for the quarantine and treatment aquariums and plastic corner filters. Keep at least four battery-powered aerators on hand for electrical failures.*

Marine animals and plants are *aerobic,* requiring oxygen to survive. During *respiration* (a term that applies to both whole organisms and their cells), oxygen is consumed and carbon dioxide is produced as a waste product. In aquariums and similar restricted environments, oxygen becomes depleted and carbon dioxide accumulates unless counteractive measures are taken. Your next decision involves the purchase of at least one air compressor and accessory components: airline tubing, gang valves, and air diffusers (Figure 4).

AIR COMPRESSORS

Air compressors supply air to the aquariums, and *airline tubing* is the conduit through which it flows. *Gang valves* regulate air flow; *air diffusers* disperse the air and enhance gas transfer (see the next section). In some respects the air compressor for the exhibit aquarium is the most important piece of equipment you will buy.

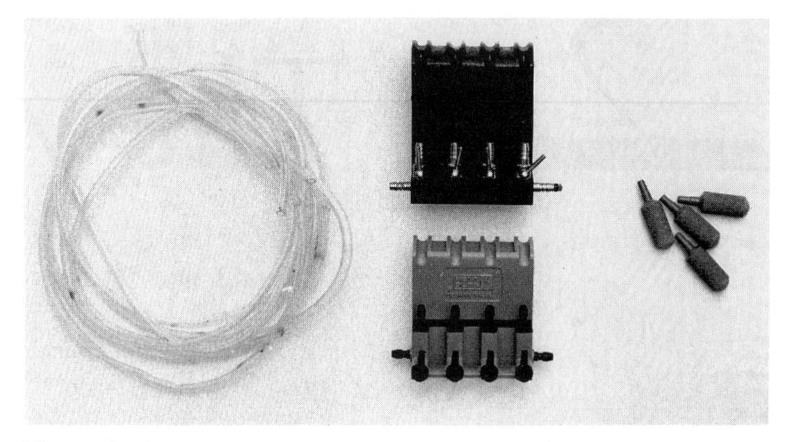

Figure 4 *Accessory components necessary to provide air to marine aquariums.* (a) *Airline tubing.* (b) *Gang valves.* (c) *Air diffusers.*

Select a good one of large capacity. Vibrator types are acceptable (Figure 5).

Sometimes a single air compressor can be rigged to service all three aquariums, but this results in an unwieldy tangle of airline tubing and gang valves, frequent adjustments to maintain consistent air flow, and no safety factor in case of malfunction. Individual units are simpler to rig, requiring less tubing and fewer valves. Most important, additional units spread the risk: If you have only one unit and it malfunctions, all your animals might die before it can be replaced. Purchase small, individual air compressors (also of the vibrator type) for the quarantine aquarium, treatment aquarium, live food container, and plastic corner filters (see Chapter 5). It is also necessary to purchase at least four battery-powered aerators in case of electrical failures. These are available from bait shops and dealers.

DIFFUSION, AERATION, GAS TRANSFER

All gases disperse by *diffusion* from higher to lower concentrations. The odor of a pungent gas such as ozone or hydrogen sulfide injected into one corner of a closed room is soon detectable everywhere as molecules[4] of the gas diffuse toward places of

[4]A *molecule,* which is composed of one or more atoms, is the smallest particle a substance can be without losing the properties that define it. An *atom* is the smallest particle of an element. An *element* is any of the more than 100 fundamental substances consisting of atoms of only one kind. Individually or in combination, elements constitute all matter in the universe.

lower concentration. Eventually they become dispersed evenly throughout the room (Figure 6). Oxygen diffuses from air into water because the concentration of oxygen in air is greater. The diffusion of oxygen into still water is slow. Compared with some other gases (for example, carbon dioxide), oxygen is only slightly soluble, meaning that it is difficult to dissolve. In addition, water

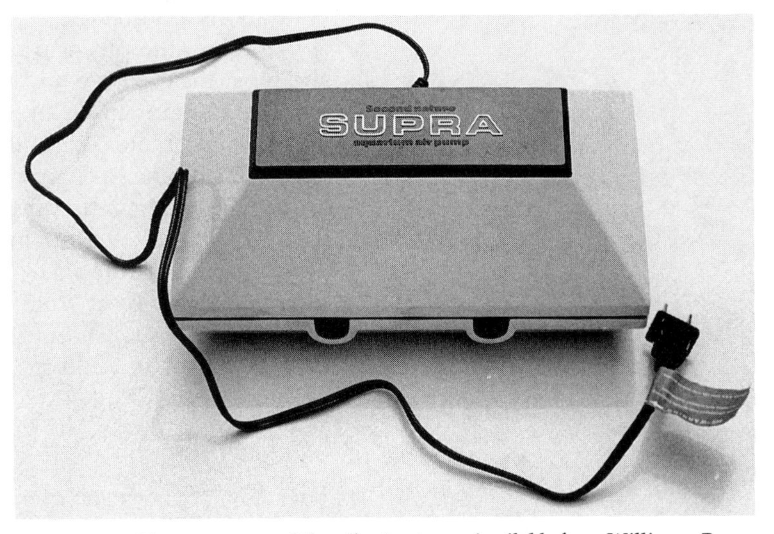

Figure 5 *Air compressor of the vibrator type. Available from Willinger Bros., Inc., Wright Way, Oakland NJ 07436. Product endorsement is not implied.*

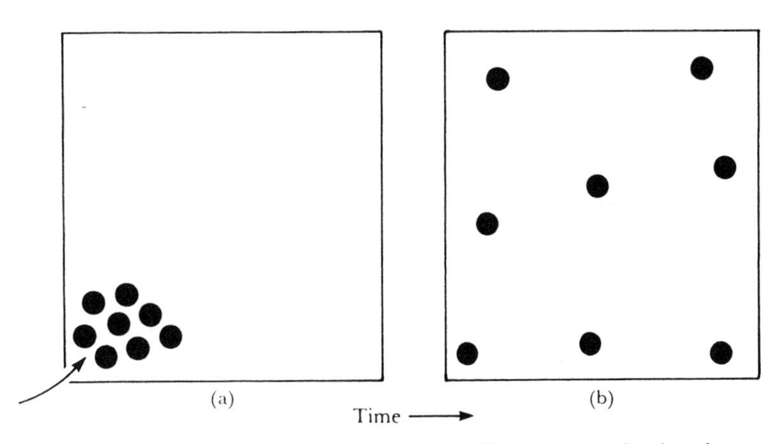

Figure 6 *Stylized illustration of molecular diffusion.* (a) *Molecules of a gas injected into one corner of a closed room are concentrated.* (b) *With time the molecules diffuse outward, eventually becoming dispersed evenly throughout the room.*

is approximately 1000 times denser than air. The first situation (low solubility) limits the amount of oxygen that can be dissolved; the second (greater density of water) limits the rate at which oxygen, once dissolved, disperses throughout the aquarium. The solubility of any gas follows natural laws that essentially are beyond the control of aquarists. However, dispersion of dissolved oxygen can be augmented by stirring, which brings depleted subsurface waters to the surface, where oxygen concentrations are greater.

Aeration—the physical process of bubbling air into water—is the most inexpensive and efficient means of stirring aquarium water and maintaining an aerobic environment (Figure 7). Its effect is to promote *gas transfer,* the process by which dissolved gases (including oxygen) are replenished from atmospheric gases originating in the air layer just above the surface of the water and from air encased in rising air bubbles. The functions of aeration are to promote oxygenation and remove excess carbon dioxide by driving it from the water into the atmosphere. The airlift pumps (see Chapter 4) provide good stirring action, and other forms of aeration are unnecessary.

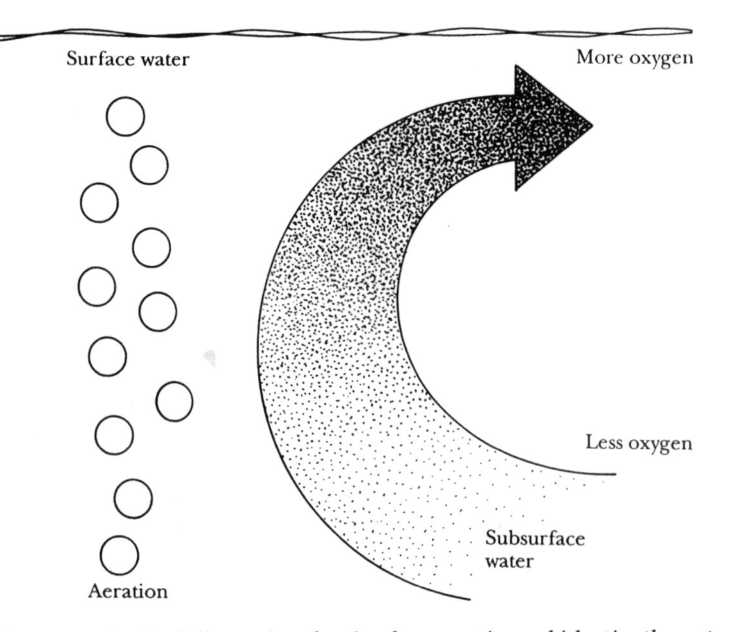

Figure 7 *Stylized illustration showing how aeration, which stirs the water, promotes an aerobic environment. Subsurface waters low in oxygen are carried to the surface, the region of greatest oxygen concentration. After being replenished with oxygen, the column of water is carried downward.*

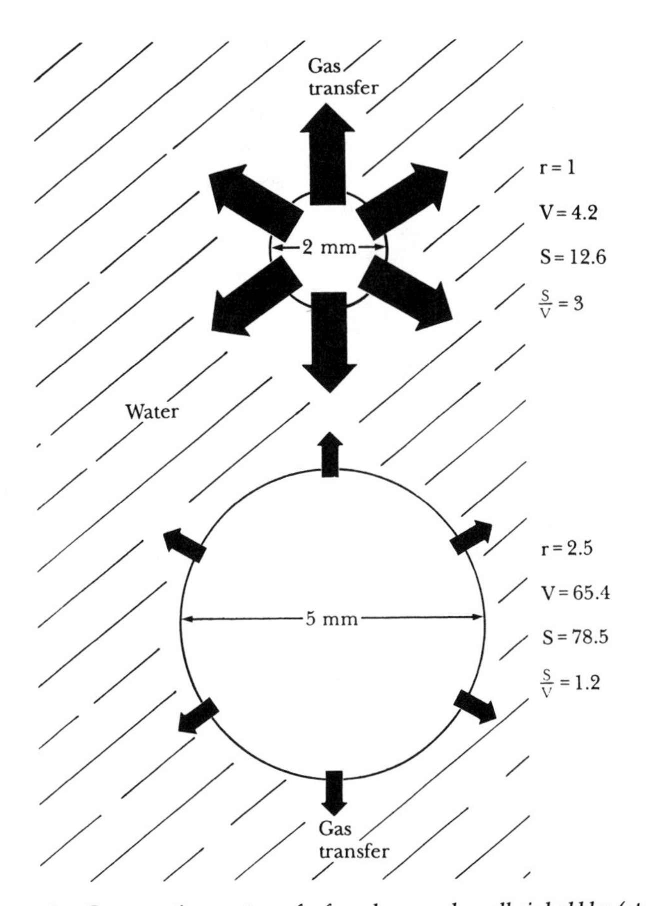

Figure 8 *Comparative gas transfer from large and small air bubbles (stylized). The surface area and volume of large bubbles exceed those of small ones, but the surface-area-to-volume ratio of small bubbles is greater. Consequently, small bubbles transfer oxygen to water more rapidly (symbolized by the larger arrows). If air bubbles are considered to be spheres, a bubble with a diameter of 2 mm (millimeters) has a surface-area-to-volume ratio 2.5 times greater than that of a bubble of 5 mm diameter.*

Most of the gas exchange in a marine aquarium takes place at the water surface, augmented by the outward transfer of gases from air bubbles rising in the lift tubes of the airlift pumps. The contribution of air bubbles to the total gas transfer can be heightened by increasing the surface areas of the bubbles while simultaneously decreasing the volumes of gas inside them. The result is to increase the *surface-area-to-volume ratio* of the air bubbles. In practice, this is accomplished by generating small bubbles instead of large ones. Gas transfer inside airlift pumps can be enhanced with air diffusers because small bubbles have larger surface-area-to-volume ratios than large bubbles (Figure 8). Consequently, a larger overall surface area is exposed to the water for gas exchange.[5]

[5]This statement is easily checked using the bubbles depicted in Figure 8. Radius, r, is half the diameter (1 and 2.5 mm for these two bubbles); other symbols are V (volume), S (surface-area), and S/V (surface-area-to-volume ratio). Formulas are $V = 4\pi r^3/3$ and $S = 4\pi r^2$; therefore, $S/V = 3/r$. In this example, respective volumes of the smaller and larger bubbles are 4.2 and 65 mm^3; respective surface areas are 12.6 and 78.5 mm^2. Respective surface-area-to-volume ratios are $S/V = 3/1 = 3\ mm^2/mm^3$, and $3/2.5 = 1.2\ mm^2/mm^3$, a disparity of 2.5 mm^2/mm^3.

CHAPTER

3 The Water

Synopsis *Either seawater or artificial seawater is suitable. Aquariums should never be filled all the way, and the final water level cannot be determined until the subgravel filter plate, gravel, and decorations have been set in place. Keep track of the amount of water added as you fill an aquarium. Make marks at regular intervals on the back corner of the outside glass surface with indelible ink indicating the cumulative volume in gallons. This step is very important. Future maintenance, treatment of diseases, and other aquarium practices require discarding and replacing fixed volumes of water. After the aquarium has been filled, also make a mark indicating the upper 25% level. This is the amount of water discarded and replaced during partial water changes. Seawater contains plankton (microscopic plants and animals) and bacteria. Many forms of plankton are detrimental to captive marine organisms, but their numbers can be reduced by aging newly collected seawater in closed plastic containers (jerry cans) for at least a week. Needed are several jerry cans with 3- to 6-gal capacities. If artificial seawater is used, large plastic garbage cans are useful mixing containers. Artificial seawater does not require aging. It can be used as soon as the salts have been dissolved. Regardless of whether you choose seawater or artificial seawater, always keep enough in reserve to administer a 25% change to the exhibit aquarium. The initial fill of water can be made directly to the new aquariums.*

You must now decide whether to use *seawater*[6] or *artificial seawater* (also called *synthetic seawater*). Artificial seawater can be prepared at home by dissolving prepackaged salts in dechlorinated tap water. The available commercial products have been blended to yield crude approximations of the main inorganic constituents found in seawater. These *artificial sea salts* (a more appropriate

[6]The term *natural seawater* is redundant because seawater is natural by definition.

artificial seawater salts) are produced by several manufacturers and sold by dealers (Figure 9). Most products are blends of dry salts, but at least one is a blend to which a little water has been added. In any case, the contents of the package must be emptied into a container of appropriate volume and dissolved in the correct amount of dechlorinated tap water. Landlocked aquarists have no choice except to use artificial seawater. If both options are available, the decision is one of convenience. Either is suitable.

Your aquariums have been purchased. Obviously, marine aquarium keeping involves the maintenance of three aquariums, not one. Only the treatment aquarium can remain empty for the moment. Plan on collecting enough seawater, or mixing enough artificial seawater, to fill the exhibit and quarantine aquariums.

The volume of water necessary to fill the aquariums initially is the largest you will ever need. Routine maintenance requires only that partial water changes be made on a regular schedule. Consequently, some aquarists prefer adding the initial fill of water directly to the new aquariums instead of transferring it from storage or mixing containers. In either case, follow the procedures provided later in this chapter.

Aquariums should never be filled all the way, and the final water level cannot be determined until the subgravel filter plate, gravel, and decorations have been set in place (see Chapters 4, 5, and 9). Keep track of the amount of water added as you fill an aquarium. Make marks at regular intervals on the back corner of the outside glass surface with indelible ink indicating the cumulative volume in gallons. This step is very important. Future maintenance, treatment of diseases, and other aquarium practices involve discarding and replacing fixed volumes of water. The surface of the water should extend to just above the bottom of the exterior decorative molding and be hidden from view (Figure 3). *After the aquarium has been filled, make a mark indicating the upper 25% level. This is the amount of water discarded and replaced during partial water changes (see Chapter 10).*

COLLECTING SEAWATER

Collect seawater in plastic *jerry cans* (Figure 10). Jerry cans are available at hardware and department stores and from suppliers of camping equipment. Purchase several with 3- to 6-gal capacities. Soak the containers in several changes of warm tap water over 12 hours to eliminate any toxic products remaining from manufacture. Do not wash them with soaps or detergents. Cleansing compounds can leave toxic residues.

Figure 9 *Artificial sea salts are produced by several manufacturers and sold by dealers. They are intended to be dissolved in an appropriate volume of dechlorinated tap water. Three representative brands are shown here. Product endorsement is not implied.* (a) *Marinemix.* (b) *Instant Ocean®.* (c) *Grande Saline Habitat®.* Sources: (a) Hawaiian Marine Imports, Inc., 10801 Kempwood, Suite 2, Houston TX 77043. (b) Aquarium Systems, 8141 Tyler Boulevard, Mentor OH 44060. (c) Argent Chemical Laboratories, 8702 152nd Avenue N.E., Redmond WA 98052.

Procedure 1 *How to Collect Seawater*

1 Attempt to collect offshore seawater. Inshore water is sometimes polluted or heavily laden with silt, plankton, and bacteria. It also might be too dilute after periods of heavy rainfall.

2 Collect from the bow of a slowly moving boat. If anchored, wait until the boat swings into the current before collecting from the bow. Both techniques lessen the possibility of entraining gasoline and other engine contaminants.

(a)

(b)

Figure 10 *Collect and store seawater in plastic jerry cans with 3- to 6-gal capacities.* (a) *These jerry cans, photographed on The University of Connecticut dock at Noank, hold 6 gal.* (b) *The culture of delicate marine animals requires unpolluted seawater. This plastic unit, which holds 1000 gal, belongs to the University of Texas Marine Biomedical Institute, located in Galveston. Researchers use it to transport and store clean seawater that has been collected several miles out in the Gulf of Mexico.*

3 Place a net over the mouth of the collecting container to strain out floating seaweed and other debris. These materials will decompose during storage and pollute the water.
4 Collect seawater after several days of calm weather. After storms or rough weather even offshore seas are turbid.
5 Store newly collected seawater in the original jerry cans with the caps screwed down tightly.

AGING SEAWATER

The sea is filled with tiny plants and animals known collectively as *plankton*. Most are microscopic (Figure 11) and drift with the currents. A few, notably the red tide organisms, release toxic compounds. Seawater also contains numerous species of bacteria, some of them pathogens of marine animals and plants. The numbers of potentially dangerous pathogens can sometimes be reduced by *aging* newly collected seawater in a sealed container. Most species of plankton die quickly in the confined space of a jerry can, slowing chemical changes in the water caused by their metabolic activities. At death their cellular contents are released. These provide nutrients for bacteria, which are able to survive in the altered environment. With time—weeks or months—

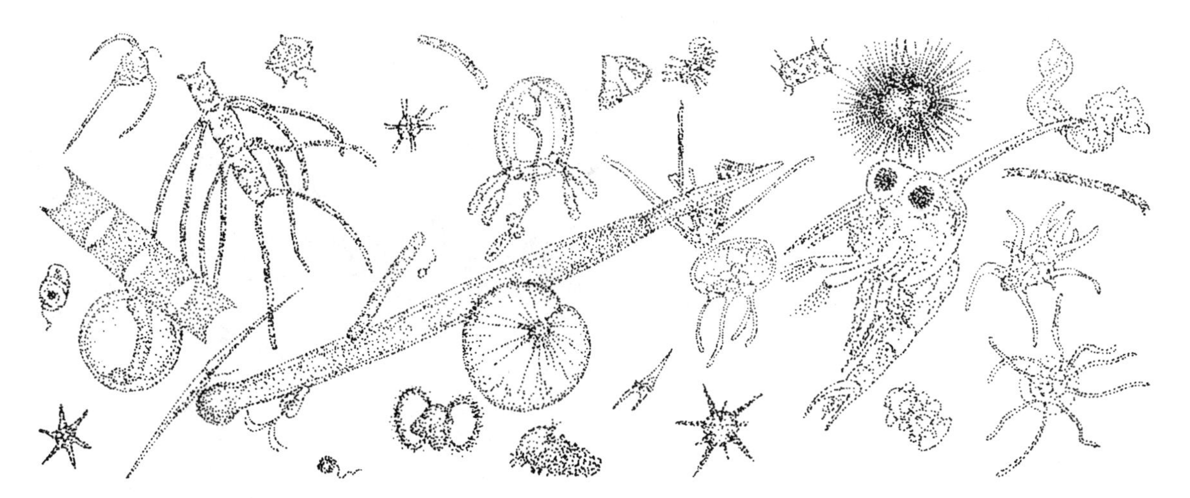

Figure 11 *Stylized illustration of tiny planktonic organisms found in seawater (magnified).* Source: S. Spotte, *Marine Aquarium Keeping: The Science, Animals, and Art*, John Wiley & Sons, Inc., © 1973, reprinted with permission.

biological and chemical factors in the water approach *steady state*, a condition of minimal change or flux. Some authors recommend that seawater be aged for several weeks before being used. Prolonged aging is inconvenient and still does not guarantee improved quality. Age newly collected seawater for at least a week. Afterward, follow Procedure 2. Always keep enough seawater available to administer a 25% change to the exhibit aquarium.

Procedure 2 *How to Prepare Seawater for Use*

1 This procedure requires an air diffuser, some airline tubing, and a small air compressor.
2 Gently move a jerry can to the drainboard of a sink. Try not to shake up the water.

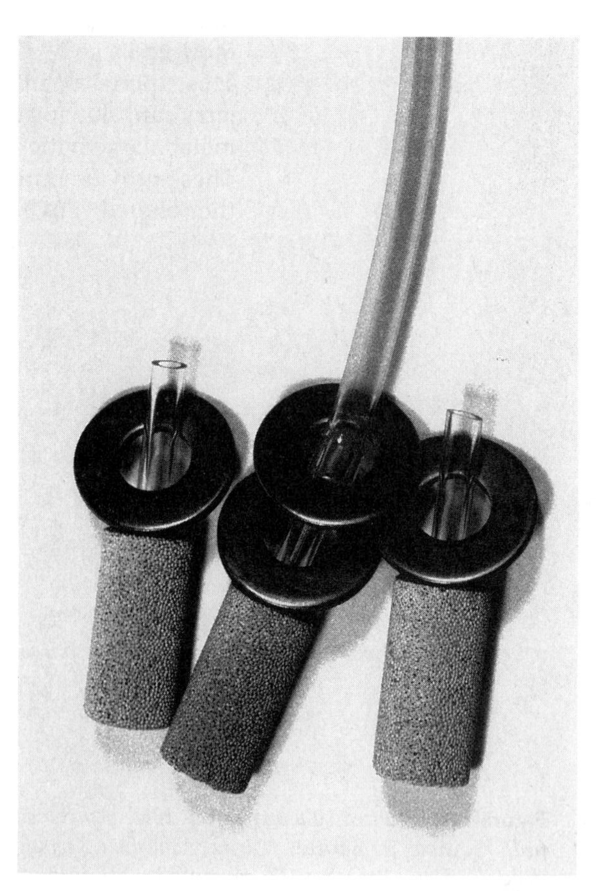

Figure 12 *Stainless steel washers (5/16-inch) are useful for weighting air diffusers. One or more can be added.*

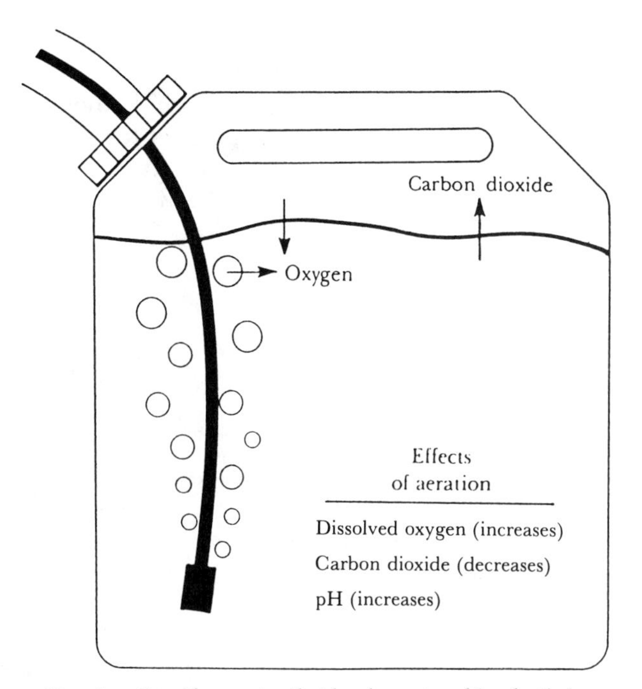

Figure 13 *Aeration of seawater that has been stored in plastic jerry cans adds oxygen and drives off excess carbon dioxide. Lowering the carbon dioxide concentration in the water raises the pH.*

3 Tilt the jerry can on one edge and siphon the silt from the bottom using a section of airline tubing. Discard the silty water (ordinarily a half-pint or less) into the sink. Siphoning techniques are described in Procedure 11 (see Chapter 10).
4 Attach the air diffuser to one end of a section of airline tubing. Attach the other end to the air compressor and plug in the unit. To be certain the air diffuser sinks to the bottom, wrap the neck with a lead strip (sold by dealers) or use two or more 5/16-inch stainless steel washers (Figure 12). These are available at hardware and marine supply stores.
5 Aerate vigorously for at least 2 hours. Aeration has beneficial effects on seawater that has been stored (Figure 13).
6 After 2 hours the water is ready to use.

DISSOLVING ARTIFICIAL SEA SALTS

If sodium chloride (one constituent of artificial sea salts) is poured into water, it starts to *dissolve,* or come apart; that is, the sodium chloride molecules separate into sodium and chloride ions[7] and begin to disperse (Figure 14). The rate at which sodium chloride and other components of artificial sea salts dissolve is a function of temperature, but the rate of dispersion can be hastened by stirring. Artificial seawaters are not fit to use until they have been dissolved completely and dispersed evenly through-

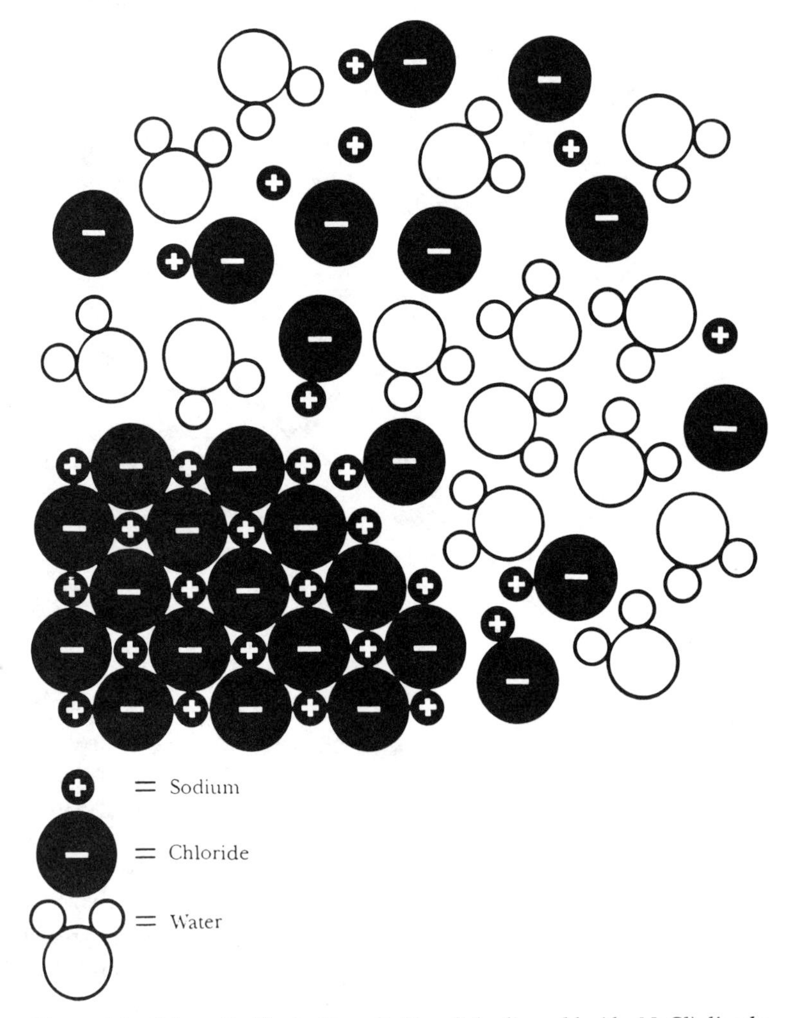

Figure 14 *Schematic illustration of table salt (sodium chloride, NaCl) dissolving. Table salt decomposes into its ionic constituents, sodium (Na^+) and chloride (Cl^-). The ions concentrate initially near the layer of undissolved salt before being surrounded by water molecules and dispersing.*

[7]An *ion* is an atom or group of atoms having a positive or negative electric charge. *Atom* is defined in text footnote 4.

out the mixing container. Aeration is the easiest method of stirring a volume of artificial seawater and dispersing its constituents evenly (Figures 15 and 16).

Artificial sea salts can be dissolved in any plastic container. New garbage cans with lids are inexpensive and convenient (Figure 17). Soak new cans for several hours in warm tap water to rid

(a) (b) (c)

Figure 15 *Aeration promotes dispersion of artificial sea salts after they have dissolved. This principle is illustrated by adding crystal violet, a dye, to three flasks of water.* (a) *The dye diffuses slowly in unaerated water because molecular diffusion is impeded by the large number of water molecules.* (b) *Dispersion is still marginal after 5 minutes.* (c) *Inserting an air diffuser disperses the dye within 5 seconds.*

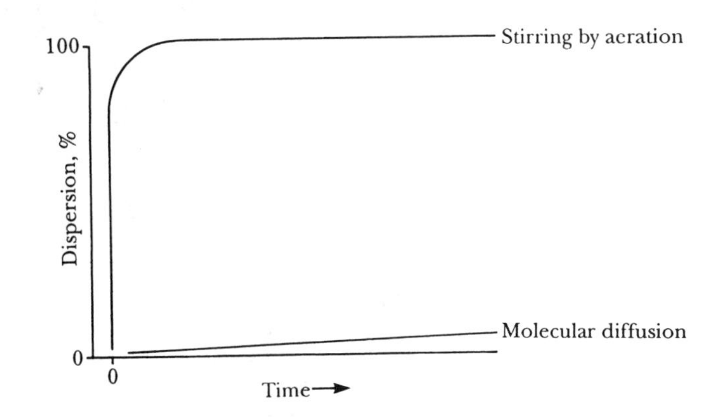

Figure 16 *Stylized graph illustrating the process in Figure 15.*

them of any potentially toxic products left from their manufacture. At least one mixing container is necessary even if all the water for the initial fill is added directly to the aquariums. Unlike seawater, artificial seawaters do not require aging. They can be used as soon as the salts have been dissolved. Always keep enough artificial seawater available to administer a 25% change to the exhibit aquarium.

Procedure 3 ***How to Dissolve Artificial Sea Salts***

1 Measure the volume of the mixing container by adding known amounts of tap water from a calibrated bucket (a

Figure 17 *Plastic garbage cans are useful for mixing artificial seawater. Calibration marks are shown on the outside. Narrower—and more accurate—marks have been made on the inside. Both sets of marks are in indelible ink.* Source: S. Spotte, *Marine Aquarium Keeping: The Science, Animals, and Art,* John Wiley & Sons, Inc., © 1973, reprinted with permission.

bucket with an embossed scale similar to a measuring cup). Mark the sides of the container at appropriate intervals with indelible ink as shown in Figure 17. Empty the container.

2. Refill the container with tap water, *but do not fill it all the way to the top.* The salts will displace some of the volume. The water should be 70 to 90°F.
3. The chlorine in tap water is toxic to marine organisms. Add the appropriate amount of a commercial dechlorinating agent (available from dealers) to remove chlorinated compounds. Base the amount added on the final volume of the mixing container.
4. Aerate for at least 2 hours to promote thorough mixing of the dechlorinating agent.
5. Read the instructions on the package of artificial sea salts and pour the salts into the mixing container. After they have dissolved, adjust the final volume by adding dechlorinated tap water.
6. If the mixing container is a plastic garbage can, drop in a length of airline tubing with an attached air diffuser and put the cover in place. To be certain the air diffuser sinks to the bottom, wrap the neck with a lead strip (sold by dealers) or use two or more 5/16-inch stainless steel washers (see Figure 12). These are available at hardware and marine supply stores.
7. If the salts have been dissolved directly in the aquariums, turn on the airlift pumps (see Chapter 4).

CHAPTER

4 The Subgravel Filter

Synopsis *A subgravel filter consists of the filter plate, gravel, and two or more airlift pumps (more commonly called airlifts). Water flowing downward through the gravel is filtered and collected in a space, or plenum, underneath the filter plate. Filtered water is circulated back to the surface by the airlifts. The continuous flow keeps most sections of the aquarium aerobic. The treatment aquarium does not need a subgravel filter.*

By itself, an aquarium filled with water is incapable of sustaining the lives of marine animals and plants. Without an apparatus designed to circulate and purify the water, captive marine environments deteriorate rapidly, dooming the inhabitants to certain death. Aquarists are offered a bewildering array of equipment purported to assist in maintaining environmental quality, but few of these items are actually necessary. All you need are subgravel filters (to be described later) for the exhibit and quarantine aquariums. The treatment aquarium does not require filtration. Buy nothing else. Many wet-dry filters, cannister filters, power filters, trickle filters, and rotating filters perform effectively under certain conditions. None, however, can match the subgravel filter for its combination of simplicity, effectiveness, ease of maintenance, and modest cost. These positive factors more than offset the negative aspects of subgravel filtration (for example, clogged air diffusers and periodic failure of the diaphragms inside the air compressors).

The subgravel filter is the central element of a marine aquarium. It purifies water circulating through a layer of gravel, rendering it suitable to sustain life. A *subgravel filter* (Figure 18) consists of three main elements: a filter plate, gravel, and two or more airlift pumps. The *filter plate*, manufactured in thin plastic, supports the gravel. The filter plate tapers downward around the periphery so that its edges fit tightly against the bottom of the aquarium. Portions of the plate are raised, forming a space, or *plenum*, underneath. Holes in the plate allow water to circulate freely through the gravel and into the plenum. If the filter plate did not have tapered edges, gravel would eventually collect in the plenum and interrupt the flow of water. A filter plate of the

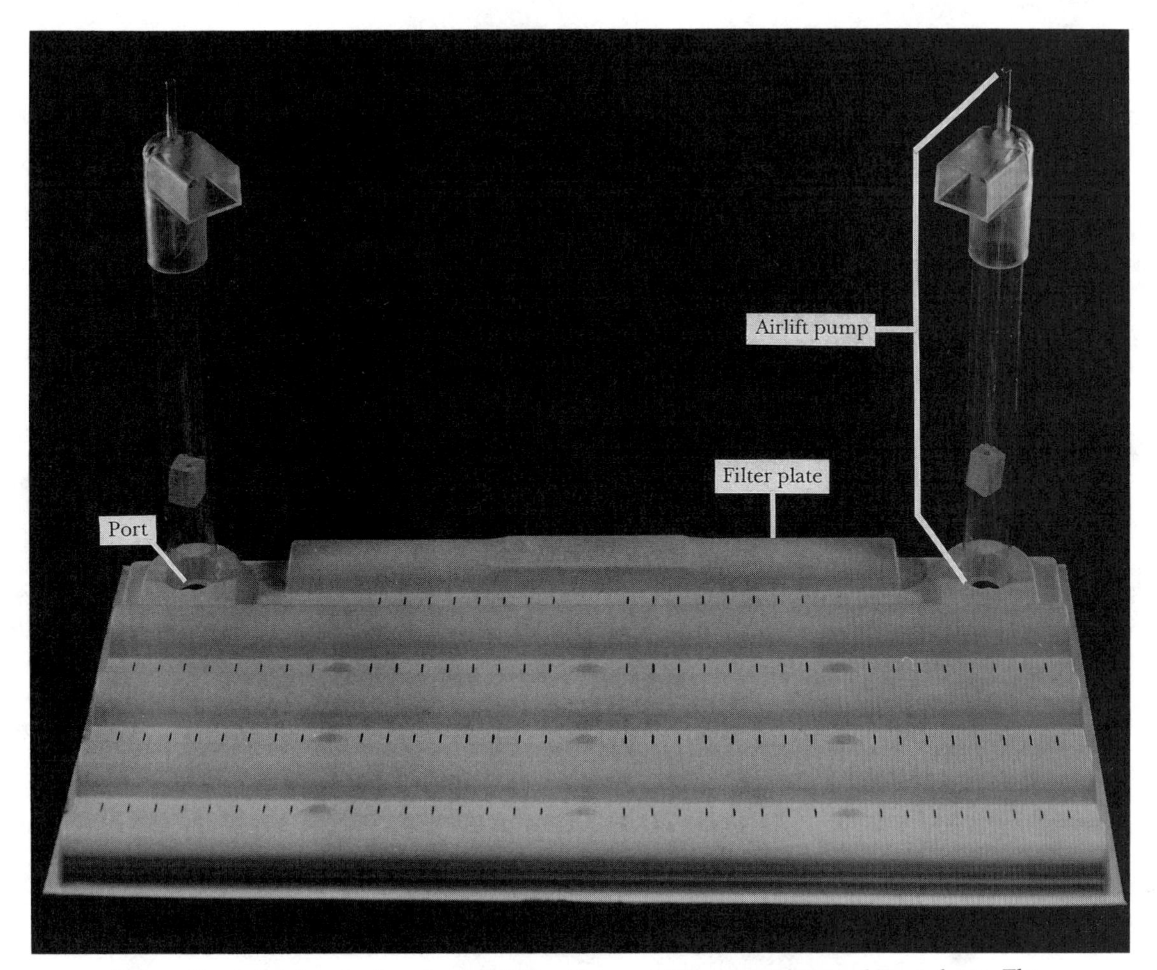

Figure 18 *Labeled parts of a subgravel filter with two airlift pumps. The gravel is not shown. The* plenum *(not shown) is located underneath raised areas of the filter plate.*

correct size is only slightly smaller than the horizontal dimensions of the aquarium so that it covers most of the bottom.

Filter plates contain *ports* (capped holes, Figure 18) designed to receive two or more *lift tubes* (Figure 19). These cylindrical tubes are parts of the *airlift pumps* (more commonly called *airlifts*). The remaining airlift pieces are the *air injection apparatus* consisting of a rigid length of plastic tubing, an *air diffuser*, and a *head piece* (Figure 19). Air injected through the air diffuser at the bottom of the lift tube causes filtered water from the plenum to be displaced upward, where it is discharged through the head piece at the surface of the aquarium (Figure 20). The continuous flow keeps most sections of the aquarium aerobic.

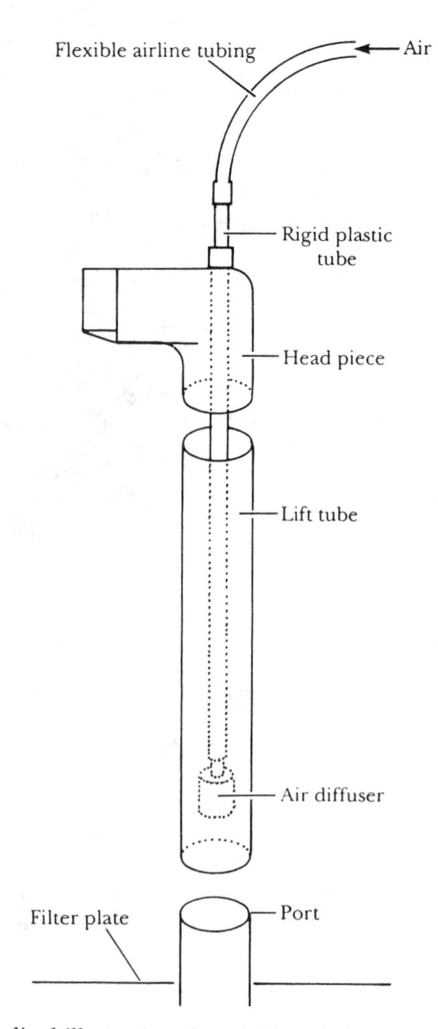

Figure 19 *Stylized illustration of an airlift with the working parts labeled.*

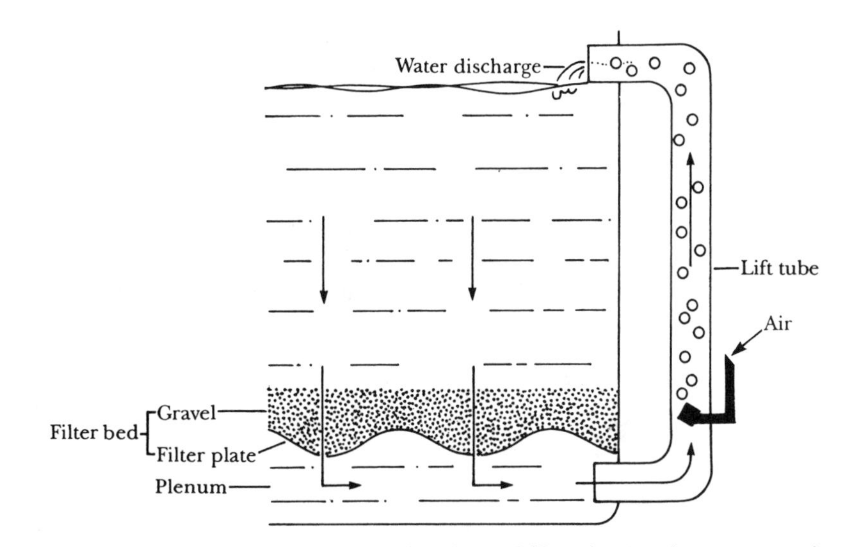

Figure 20 *Stylized illustration of a subgravel filter showing the movement of water.* Source: Modified from S. Spotte, *Fish and Invertebrate Culture: Water Management in Closed Systems,* Second edition, John Wiley & Sons, Inc., © 1979, reprinted with permission.

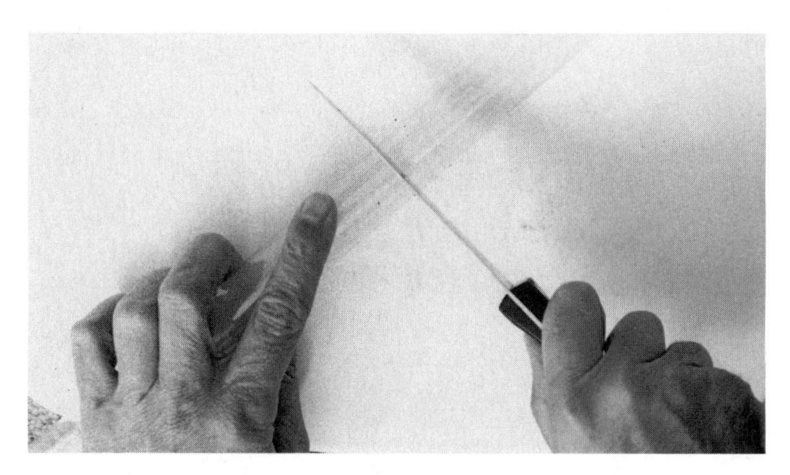

Figure 21 *Cut lift tubes to the proper length with a hacksaw or serrated kitchen knife. The water level should be located at the lower lip of the head piece of the airlift (see Figure 19).*

Most filter plates can accept at least two lift tubes, one at each back corner. Filter plates designed for larger aquariums have additional ports along the back edge. The quarantine aquarium and exhibit aquariums up to 50 gal require only two lift tubes even if additional ports are available. Use three lift tubes to aquariums of 50 to 75 gal, and four in aquariums larger than 75 gal. If the lift tubes are too long, cut them to proper lengths with a serrated kitchen knife or a hacksaw (Figure 21). When a lift tube has been sectioned to the proper length, the bottom lip of the head piece is just below the surface of the water. The exact lengths are difficult to determine in an empty aquarium. *Do not cut the lift tubes until the filter gravel has been added and leveled (see Chapter 5), the decorations set in place (see Chapter 9), and the water level raised until hidden from view by the exterior decorative molding around the top of the aquarium (see Chapter 3).*

CHAPTER

5 The Gravel

Synopsis *Gravel on a filter plate is the filtrant. Its functions are to (1) maintain water clarity by trapping suspended particulate matter, (2) provide attachment sites for beneficial filter bacteria that convert ammonia and nitrite, and (3) assist in a limited way with alkalinity and pH control. Alkalinity is the sum of chemical compounds present to neutralize acids; pH is a measure of the acidity or basicity of the water. When leveled, the gravel should be at least 2 inches deep and cover the entire filter plate. Ammonia is toxic to marine animals. Sources of ammonia are (1) the animals themselves, which excrete it as a waste product; and (2) the breakdown of organic compounds in the water by filter bacteria. Still other filter bacteria convert ammonia to nitrite and nitrate, which are less toxic. Most biochemical processes in aquariums are aerobic and therefore acid forming. Seawater and artificial seawaters, however, are slightly basic, a condition that must be maintained in marine aquariums. The most important constituent of the alkalinity is bicarbonate. It constitutes a reservoir that neutralizes acidic compounds and keeps the pH on the basic side of neutral. The alkalinity, and ultimately the pH, depend on an adequate reservoir of bicarbonate dissolved in the water. The ideal pH of a marine aquarium is 8.2. To prevent the alkalinity from being depleted initially, rinse new gravel thoroughly with tap water, then soak it for 24 hours in a little seawater or artificial seawater. Discard this water before filling the aquarium. Much of the organic material in marine aquariums exists as aggregates or particles; the rest is dissolved organic carbon, which raises the overall metabolic activity of the aquarium and imparts a greenish-yellow color to the water. Dissolved organic carbon is removed rapidly and efficiently with activated carbon (1 oz per 25 gal of aquarium water) packed into a corner filter. Operate activated carbon filters every other day. Some activated carbons (especially those manufactured from coal) appear to cause minor skin and gill irritation in fishes if used continuously. Replace the material every 2 weeks and more often if the water remains greenish yellow after treatment.*

You must next decide on the gravel for the subgravel filters of the exhibit and quarantine aquariums. Select a carbonate mineral that has been crushed and graded more or less to uniform size (Figure 22). The most common materials are oyster shell, coral, "coral hash," and dolomite. Coral hash is sometimes preferable for reasons given in Chapter 13, but availability often dictates the choice. Crushed oyster shell is sold at feed stores for poultry grit. Dolomite can be purchased at plant nurseries. Crushed coral and coral hash are sometimes available from dealers. *Coral hash* is a composite of pulverized coral rubble, coral sand, broken shells, and other nonspecific materials.

Gravel spread on the filter plate acts as a *filtrant*; the water, which is the substance being filtered, is the *filtrate*. Gravel as a filtrant serves three critical functions. First, during normal circulation the gravel grains assist with maintaining water clarity by sieving out suspended particles that cause turbidity (Figure 23). Particulate matter is trapped and concentrated in the spaces between grains for easier removal during routine maintenance. In this sense the gravel functions as a *mechanical filter*. Second, the surfaces of the gravel soon become populated by filter bacteria that convert toxins released by the animals and plants to harmless or less toxic compounds. This function is *biological filtration*. Clearly, a well-managed marine aquarium is one in which the filter bacteria flourish. Third, filtrants composed of carbonate

Figure 22 *This 1965 photograph shows coral gravel being graded by shoveling it onto a series of screens of decreasing mesh size. Only gravel of uniform size retained on the bottom screen was kept. The material was shipped to Niagara Falls, New York, where it was placed in the subgravel filters of a public aquarium under construction. Aquarium of Niagara Falls opened in June 1965 and was the first public aquarium to use artificial seawater exclusively. Much of the original material is still in place.* Source: Jessop Smith.

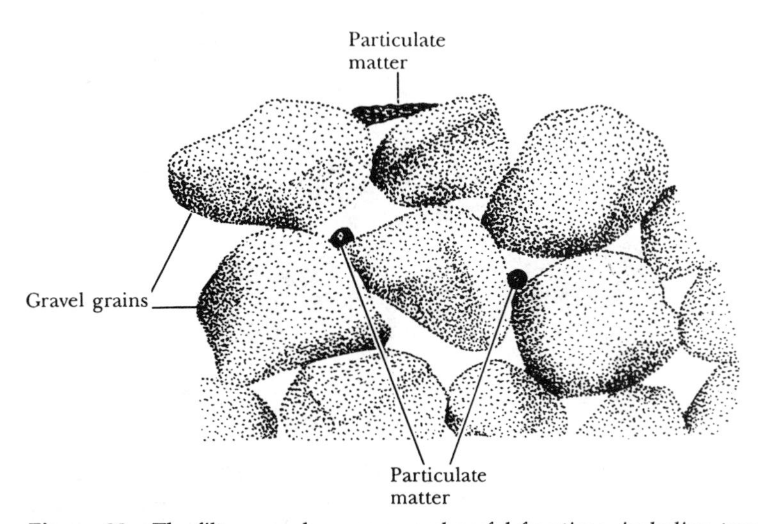

Figure 23 *The filter gravel serves several useful functions, including trapping and concentrating particulate matter so that it can be removed during routine maintenance.* Sources: George Tchobanoglous, Department of Civil Engineering, University of California at Davis, reprinted with permission; also modified from S. Spotte, *Marine Aquarium Keeping: The Science, Animals, and Art*, John Wiley & Sons, Inc., © 1973, reprinted with permission.

minerals help keep the aquarium environment slightly basic, or similar in this respect to ocean water.

As mentioned previously, pulverized coral rubble is a component of coral hash. However, the natural (unpulverized) material should also be of interest to marine aquarists. By definition, *coral rubble* comprises broken, irregular pieces of dead coral worn smooth by abrasion. Few dealers stock it, which is unfortunate. Used alone, coral rubble is a poor filtrant because of its large size, although a layer of it spread over a true filtrant (for example, coral gravel or coral hash) does not impair subgravel filtration. When applied in this way, coral rubble provides a natural substratum for many species of small, bottom-dwelling fishes and invertebrates that occupy the shallow waters around coral reefs (see Chapter 13; also see Color Plates 2c, 7a, 7c, 8b, and 14b).

ESTIMATING THE AMOUNT OF GRAVEL NEEDED

Filtrants ordinarily are sold by the pound. However, the weights of carbonate mineral gravels differ. Procedure 4 explains how to estimate the amounts needed of four common gravels—oyster

Figure 24 *Four filtrants used in marine aquariums. Only one is required. The ruler shows approximate grain sizes in millimeters.* (a) *Coral gravel.* (b) *Coral hash.* (c) *Oyster shell.* (d) *Dolomite.*

shell, coral, coral hash, and dolomite (Figure 24)—based on their approximate *densities*, or weights per volume (Table 2). The values of some materials might vary from the tabular values, depending on how carefully the material has been sieved. Of the materials listed, coral hash is likely to vary the most because it consists of more than one component. *The gravel should be at least 2 inches deep and cover the entire filter plate.*

Procedure 4 ***How to Estimate the Amount of Gravel***

1 Select one of the gravels listed above. Few dealers carry all four.

2 Calculate the volume of filtrant by multiplying the inside length and width of the aquarium in inches by 2 (the recommended minimum depth in inches).

TABLE 2 Densities of common marine aquarium filtrants at stated grain size ranges. Standard deviation of three replicate samples is shown in parentheses.

Filtrant	Size Range, mm	Density, g/cm^3	Density, lb/in^3
Oyster shell	1–12	1.05 ($\pm$0.03)	0.038 ($\pm$0.001)
Coral	3–6	1.05 ($\pm$0.04)	0.038 ($\pm$0.002)
Coral hash	1–9	1.25 ($\pm$0.02)	0.045 ($\pm$0.001)
Dolomite	2–5	1.36 ($\pm$0.01)	0.049 ($\pm$0.000)

Source: Patricia M. Bubucis, Sea Research Foundation and Marine Sciences Institute, The University of Connecticut.

3 Multiply the value obtained in step 2 by the appropriate density (for example, by 0.045 lb/in^3 for coral hash).
4 *Example:* The inside dimensions of the aquarium are 20 inches by 10 inches. Coral hash is the filtrant. To obtain the volume of filtrant needed in cubic inches (in^3), multiply the length and width of the aquarium by filtrant depth:

$$20 \text{ inches} \times 10 \text{ inches} \times 2 \text{ inches} = 400\,\text{in}^3$$

To obtain the weight of filtrant needed, multiply the volume obtained by the density of the material selected (for example, coral hash):

$$400\,\cancel{\text{in}^3} \times 0.045\,\text{lb}/\cancel{\text{in}^3} = 18\,\text{lb of coral hash}$$

BIOLOGICAL FILTRATION

With age, aquarium gravel acquires a population of resident filter bacteria. Many of these are important in promoting a healthy aquarium environment, as described shortly. In large measure, the survival of captive fishes, invertebrates, and plants depends directly on a thriving population of filter bacteria. Both aerobic and anaerobic bacteria can be found in marine aquariums. *Aerobes* require oxygen; *anaerobes* are able to carry out their metabolic processes in the absence of oxygen. Aerobic forms assume greater importance because aquariums are predominantly aerobic environments.

Filter bacteria live inside thin, self-secreted layers of slime on the surfaces of gravel grains. To reach individual bacterial cells, oxygen and nutrients must diffuse inward through the biological slime layer (Figure 25). Waste products diffuse outward into the

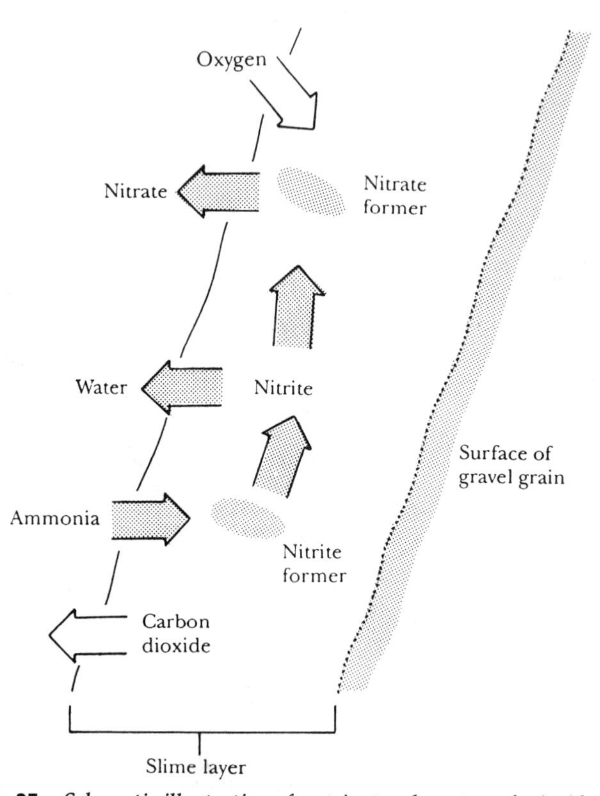

Figure 25 *Schematic illustration of nutrient and gas transfer inside a biological slime layer. These layers form on the surfaces of gravel grains in the subgravel filter. Oxygen and ammonia diffuse inward. Ammonia is oxidized to nitrite by nitrifying bacteria that are nitrite formers. Other nitrifiers (the nitrate formers) then oxidize nitrite to nitrate. Some of the nitrite and most of the nitrate diffuse into the water.*

water. Rapid movement of water through the filtrant enhances both inward and outward diffusion by lowering the concentrations of oxygen and waste products at the slime surfaces.

Among the numerous groups of beneficial aerobic bacteria in aquariums are the *nitrifiers,* which convert ammonia to nitrite and ultimately nitrate by the biochemical process of *nitrification* (Figures 25 and 26). Fishes and most other marine animals are *ammonotelic;* that is, they produce *ammonia* as the principal nitrogenous waste product of protein metabolism (proteins are approximately 16% nitrogen). In fishes, the gills are the principal site of ammonia excretion (Figure 26). Ammonia is toxic to marine animals (Table 3), and its control is an important aspect of managing a marine aquarium. Ammonia released into the vast reaches of the sea dissipates quickly, seldom reaching toxic con-

TABLE 3 Effects of toxic concentrations of ammonia to fishes.

Extensive damage to tissues, especially gill and kidney tissues
Physiological imbalances
Impaired growth
Decreased resistance to disease
Increased susceptibility to predation

centrations. However, ammonia released into a marine aquarium can accumulate, presenting the possibility of the animals being poisoned by their own wastes. *The primary function of nitrification in marine aquariums is ammonia conversion.*

During nitrification, one group of nitrifiers—the nitrite formers—metabolizes aqueous ammonia and converts it to nitrite, a far less toxic compound (see Figure 25). A second group—the nitrate formers—metabolizes nitrite to produce nitrate, which is even less toxic than nitrite. The nitrate concentration is lowered by dilution during routine partial water changes (see Chapter 10).

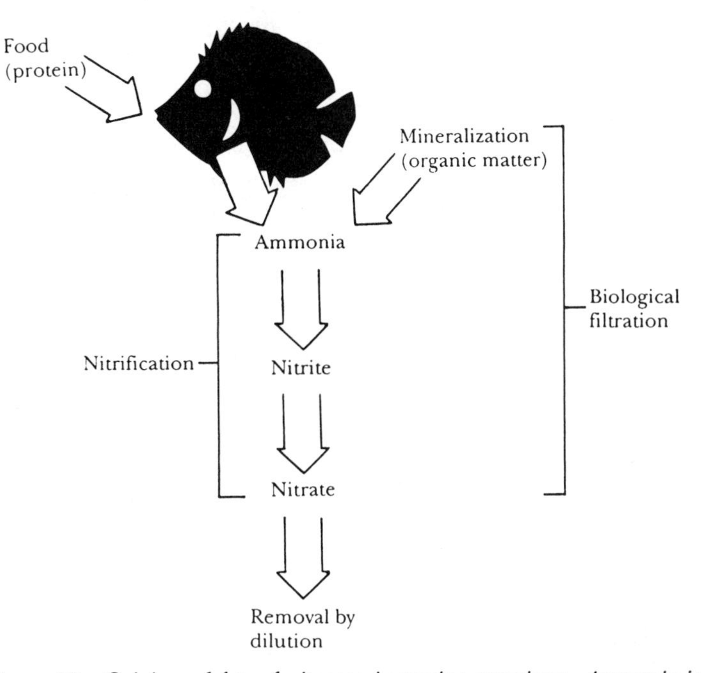

Figure 26 *Origin and fate of nitrogen in marine aquariums. Ammonia is a product of protein metabolism and excreted by aquarium animals as a waste product. It also is formed during the mineralization of organic matter by bacteria. Ammonia is then oxidized to nitrite, which in turn is oxidized to nitrate, both processes by nitrifying bacteria.* Biological filtration *is the sum of mineralization and nitrification.*

Ammonia enters aquarium water from a second source, the *mineralization* or breakdown of organic matter by a diverse array of mostly aerobic bacteria known as *heterotrophs*. Unlike the nitrifiers, heterotrophs ordinarily require organic forms of nitrogen and carbon. Organic matter in aquarium water has several sources. Some organic compounds are released by algae; others appear routinely when filter bacteria die and rupture, spilling their cellular contents into the water. The remaining sources are leftover food and animal wastes. Many heterotrophs live in slime layers that coat gravel grains, but numerous others are suspended in the water. The fate of ammonia produced by mineralization is the same as that released directly by animals: Nitrifying bacteria convert it first to nitrite and then to nitrate. Together, mineralization and nitrification make up *biological filtration* (Figure 26).

ALKALINITY AND pH

As mentioned previously, the pH of the oceans is slightly basic. The seawater or artificial seawater of a marine aquarium must be maintained in a similar state. The terms *acidic* and *basic* are used in reference to the *pH scale*, which ranges from 0 to 14. At pH 7 a substance is neither acidic nor basic; it is *neutral*. Basic and acidic substances have pH values that are, respectively, greater and less than neutral (Figure 27). The typical pH of ocean waters is 8.2, the same value recommended for marine aquariums.

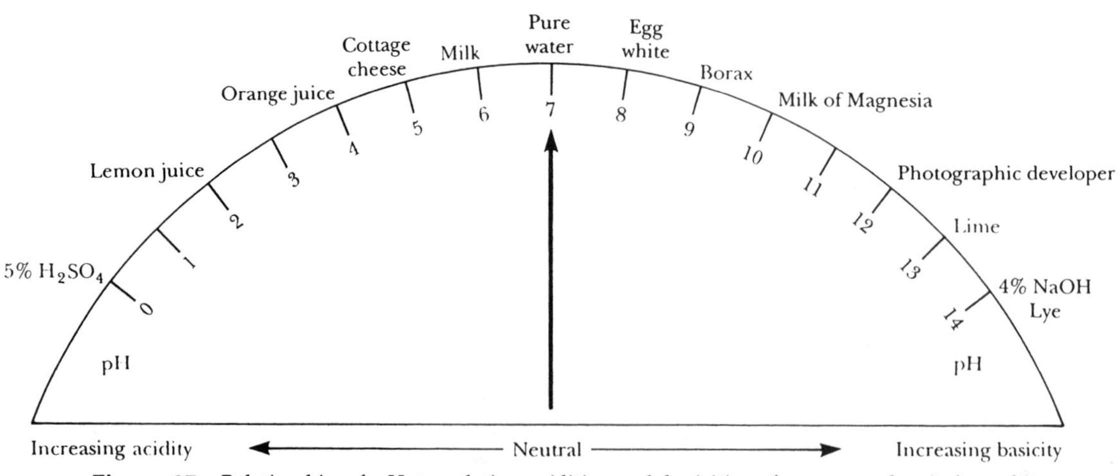

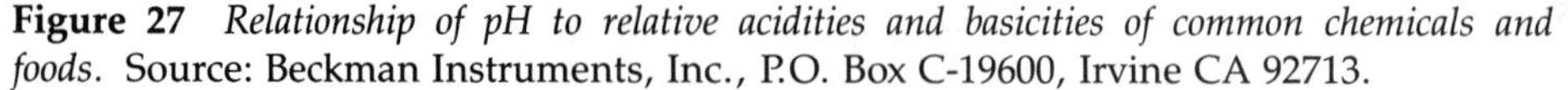

Figure 27 *Relationship of pH to relative acidities and basicities of common chemicals and foods.* Source: Beckman Instruments, Inc., P.O. Box C-19600, Irvine CA 92713.

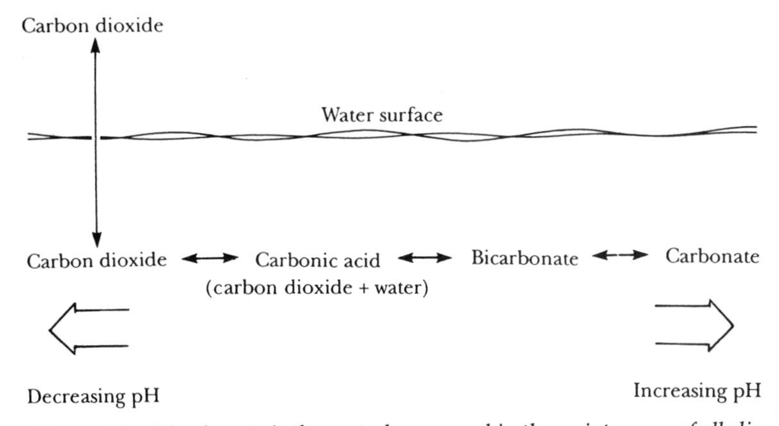

Figure 28 *Bicarbonate is the central compound in the maintenance of alkalinity. Carbon dioxide (CO_2) passes across the surface of the water in both directions. It reacts with water (H_2O) to form carbonic acid (H_2CO_3). A shift toward formation of bicarbonate (HCO_3^-) and carbonate (CO_3^{2-}) results in a pH increase. A shift in the direction of carbon dioxide causes the pH to decline.*

The pH of marine aquarium water is controlled by the *alkalinity,* defined as the sum of chemical compounds that neutralize acids. Alkalinity is the factor that maintains aquarium water on the basic side of neutral. The pH of aquarium water diminishes with time as acidic compounds accumulate. Carbon dioxide, a waste product of aerobic metabolism, reacts with water molecules to form carbonic acid. Other acidic substances enter aquarium water as a result of animal, plant, and bacterial metabolism and accumulate with time. Even nitrification produces acids.

In seawater and artificial seawaters the most important constituent of the alkalinity is *bicarbonate.* It neutralizes acidic compounds, keeping the pH basic (Figure 28). Thus the alkalinity—and ultimately the pH—depends on an adequate reservoir of bicarbonate dissolved in the water. Over time, tiny amounts of carbonate material, deposited on the surfaces of carbonate mineral filtrants, dissolve. The released carbonate then reacts with other constituents in the water to form bicarbonate. Carbonate minerals help prevent the pH from falling lower than approximately 7.8, but they do not, in themselves, sustain pH values above the minimum recommended threshold of 8.0. Alkalinity and pH are discussed in greater detail in Chapter 6, and methods of their control are covered in Chapter 10.

A curious event occurs when gravel grains composed of carbonate minerals are placed initially in seawater or artificial seawater. Logically, the grains should dissolve slowly until their surfaces become covered by biological slime and other contaminants. But this is not what happens. Instead, calcium and magnesium combine with carbonate to form coatings on the gravel grains, covering their surfaces with compounds similar in composition to the minerals themselves (Figure 29). As just mentioned, components of the new surface coatings derive originally from the water. In fact, when dissolved they make up a portion of the alkalinity. The result is that new carbonate mineral filtrants initially *remove* alkalinity from aquarium water, reducing the amount of bicarbonate and tending to lower the pH of new marine aquariums.

The abrupt loss of alkalinity in a new aquarium can be prevented by precoating the mineral surfaces before adding the water. This is done by rinsing the filtrant in tap water to get rid of excessive dust (Figure 30), followed by soaking the material in a little new seawater or artificial seawater for 24 hours. Soaking allows natural surface coatings to form on the gravel surfaces as calcium, magnesium, and carbonate are removed from the surrounding water. Afterward, the soak water, minus much of its alkalinity, is discarded. The aquarium can then be filled.

Procedure 5 ***How to Precoat New Carbonate Mineral Gravels***

1. Rinse the gravel thoroughly with tap water to remove dust.
2. Soak the gravel in seawater or artificial seawater for at least 24 hours. Add water to a depth of 4 inches above the top of the gravel. Soaking can be done in a bucket or directly in the aquarium. *If the newly rinsed gravel is placed directly in an aquarium to be soaked, install the lift tubes of the airlifts (see Figure 19) or leave the caps covering the ports of the subgravel filter plate in place (see Figure 18); otherwise, much of the gravel will be flushed into the plenum underneath the filter plate.*
3. After 24 hours discard the water. Do not rinse again with tap water.
4. Fill the aquarium with new seawater or artificial seawater.

CONTROL OF DISSOLVED ORGANIC CARBON

Much of the organic material in marine aquariums exists as aggregates or particles, some large enough to be visible. The rest, which is dissolved (that is, present in molecular or ionic states), is referred to by oceanographers as *dissolved organic carbon*. Most of the dissolved organic carbon is colorless, but some compounds contain pigments that impart an unsightly greenish-yellow appearance to the water.

Figure 29 *Overgrowths form quickly on new carbonate minerals placed in seawater or artificial seawater. Their formation is accompanied by loss of alkalinity from the surrounding water. These photographs, taken through a scanning electron microscope, depict the formation of magnesian calcite overgrowths on pure calcite crystals in artificial seawater of pH 8.40 (other conditions not stated here). Magnesian calcite and pure calcite are carbonate minerals.* (a) *Pure calcite at the start of the experiment (magnified 7875 times).* (b) *Magnesian calcite overgrowths on pure calcite after 10 to 50 hours (magnified 8250 times). To avoid initial loss of alkalinity in new marine aquariums, soak carbonate minerals for 24 hours under 4 inches or so of new seawater or artificial seawater.* Source: Reprinted with permission from R. A. Berner, The role of magnesium in the crystal growth of calcite and aragonite from sea water, *Geochimica et Cosmochimica Acta* 39: 489-504, © 1975, Pergamon Press, Ltd.

Figure 30 *Rinse new filtrants in flowing tap water to get rid of excess dust before soaking them in seawater or artificial seawater.* Source: S. Spotte, *Marine Aquarium Keeping: The Science, Animals, and Art,* John Wiley & Sons, Inc., © 1973, reprinted with permission.

The pigmented portion of the dissolved organic carbon has several sources, including the contents of ruptured bacterial cells. Many of the substances released are pigmented or react with other compounds to produce pigmented molecules. Additional pigmented compounds form during the mineralization of leftover food and animal wastes; still others are liberated by algae attached to the gravel, decorations, and inside surfaces of the aquarium glass.

Heterotrophic bacteria increase in numbers as the concentration of dissolved organic carbon accumulates, and their metabolic activities hasten the decline in alkalinity and pH. These and other events associated with deterioration of the environment make intermittent removal of organic compounds from the water necessary. *The first reason for removing dissolved organic carbon is cosmetic (to reduce the intensity of the greenish-yellow color of the water); the second is biological (to lower the overall metabolic activity of the aquarium).*

Dissolved organic carbon can be removed with activated carbon. Some authors use the terms *activated carbon* and *charcoal* interchangeably, but this is incorrect; the two substances are different.

The pores of activated carbon trap dissolved organic carbon molecules rapidly and efficiently (Figure 31). Activated carbons are manufactured from products such as animal bones, wood, and coal. Animal bones are by-products of the meat packing industry. The only apparatus required to hold activated carbon is a simple plastic corner filter powered by air (Figure 32). The exhibit aquarium should always be equipped with such a filter, as should the quarantine aquarium when it contains animals. Corner filters are available in different sizes, although size is of minor importance, provided the units hold enough activated carbon (see the next paragraph). *Do not buy a foam fractionator (also called a protein skimmer) or an ozone generator. Neither device is necessary to control dissolved organic carbon efficiently, and both are more difficult to operate than a corner filter.*

The corner filter is filled with rinsed activated carbon sandwiched between layers of quilt batting (sold at fabric supply stores) or filter fiber. Quilt batting is preferable because it can be rinsed and reused. *Use 1 oz (dry weight) of activated carbon per 25 gal*

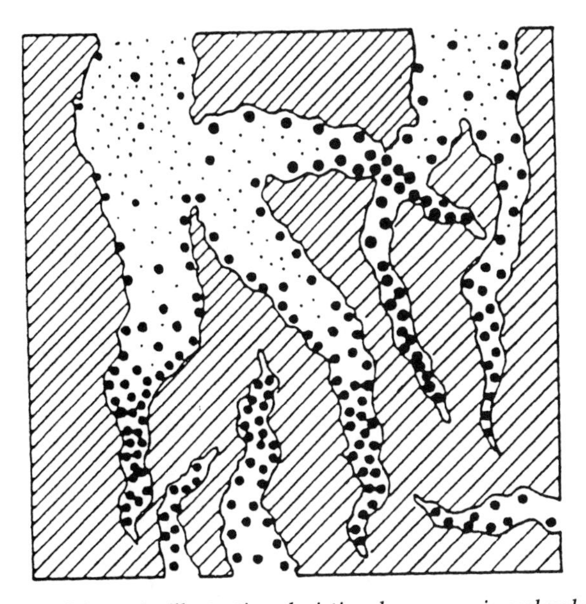

Figure 31 *Schematic illustration depicting how organic molecules become trapped in the pores of activated carbon. The material is removed from the aquarium when the activated carbon is discarded.* Source: Barnebey and Sutcliffe Corp., P.O. Box 2526, Columbus OH 43216.

Figure 32 *Activated carbon (left) is placed in a corner filter (right) powered by air and held in place with quilt batting (center) or filter fiber (not shown). Quilt batting is preferable because it can be rinsed and used again. Product endorsement is not implied.*

of aquarium water. Operate activated carbon filters (see Procedure 6) every other day. Some activated carbons (especially those manufactured from coal) appear to cause minor skin and gill irritation in fishes if used continuously. Turn off the flow of air every other day to cease operation, but leave the unit in place.

Some kinds of activated carbon remain viable for several weeks before reaching *saturation,* a state in which the pores can no longer hold additional dissolved organic carbon. However, viability declines steadily with time. Saturation has been reached if the water is still pigmented after treatment. *Replace activated carbon every 2 weeks and more often if the water remains greenish yellow after treatment.*

Procedure 6 ***How to Use an Activated Carbon Filter***

1 Rinse an appropriate amount of activated carbon to remove most of the black carbon dust. This is easily done by emptying the material into a coarse-mesh net and rinsing it under the tap. The net will be blackened permanently and should not be used for other purposes. *Activated carbon also removes organic compounds from air. Store the remaining material only after closing the container tightly to prevent accumulation of air pollutants.*

2 Open the lid of the corner filter and remove the inside stem with its attached flange. With scissors, cut a thin piece of

quilt batting and place it in the very bottom of the corner filter.

3 Replace the stem and fill the corner filter with the wet activated carbon.

4 Cut a piece of quilt batting to fit tightly into the top of the corner filter (that is, between the surface of the activated carbon and the lid). The top and bottom layers of batting prevent any remaining black carbon dust from leaking into the aquarium. Also insert a plug of quilt batting in the empty chamber adjacent to the one now filled with activated carbon.

5 Connect the corner filter to an air compressor with a length of airline tubing.

6 Adjust the air flow to provide steady aeration. Use gang valves if necessary.

7 Place the filter in a corner of the aquarium or behind one of the decorations (see Chapter 9).

8 Replace activated carbon in the filter every 2 weeks, or sooner if the water is still pigmented after treatment. Discard the used material. At the same time, remove the quilt batting and clean it by holding it under the tap and squeezing it several times.

CHAPTER

6 The New Environment

Synopsis *The exhibit and quarantine aquariums will be unfit to support life until their subgravel filters have been aged or conditioned for approximately 3 weeks. In a conditioned subgravel filter first ammonia and then nitrite have reached their maximum concentrations (that is, they have peaked) and begun to decline. A subgravel filter is considered fully conditioned when the nitrite concentration has declined to almost zero. At temperatures above 70°F, this occurs in 2 months or less. The function of a conditioned subgravel filter is to (1) convert organic matter and inorganic nitrogen generated by the animals, plants, and bacteria to less objectionable chemical forms; and (2) maintain ammonia at concentrations too small to be determined with aquarium test kits. Conditioning can be accelerated by "seeding" the new subgravel filter at home with gravel from a dealer's aquarium or by addition of packaged nitrifiers. Neither practice is recommended. The first can transmit infectious diseases; the second is often ineffective. Condition new subgravel filters with a commercial ammonium salt or salt solution. The acceptable alkalinity range in a marine aquarium is 2.5 to 3.0 milliequivalents per liter (mEq/L). The acceptable pH range is 8.0 to 8.3; the ideal value is 8.2. Heavy aeration by airlift pumping, which drives off excess carbon dioxide, is the most effective means of sustaining pH values above 8.0. Select a pH test kit designed for use with marine aquariums. Test kits designed to determine pH in freshwater will give false readings. Specific gravity is the ratio of the density of seawater or artificial seawater to the density of pure water. The density of a substance is its weight per volume. The density of pure water is 1.000 gram per cubic centimeter (g/cm^3). Seawater is approximately 2.5% denser than pure water. Marine aquarium waters should have specific* *gravity values within the range 1.023 to 1.025 at 80°F. If adjustments in pH or specific gravity are necessary, consult Chapter 10.*

Before adding animals to the quarantine and exhibit aquariums you must make certain the water is chemically suitable. A new aquarium is like the surface of the moon: sterile, forbidding, and unfit to support life. This is the situation until the subgravel filter has been aged or *conditioned* for approximately 3 weeks. Management decisions—both now and later—will be based partly on analyses of alkalinity, pH, specific gravity, and three forms of nitrogen: ammonia, nitrite, and nitrate. After reading this chapter you must purchase the appropriate *test kits* and a *hydrometer* to determine specific gravity. You also will need one or more submersible *immersion heaters* and *thermometers* (Figure 33) to be left permanently in each aquarium. Immersion heaters will be described shortly. It is not necessary to determine ammonia, nitrite, and nitrate when the aquarium is first set up. Nonetheless,

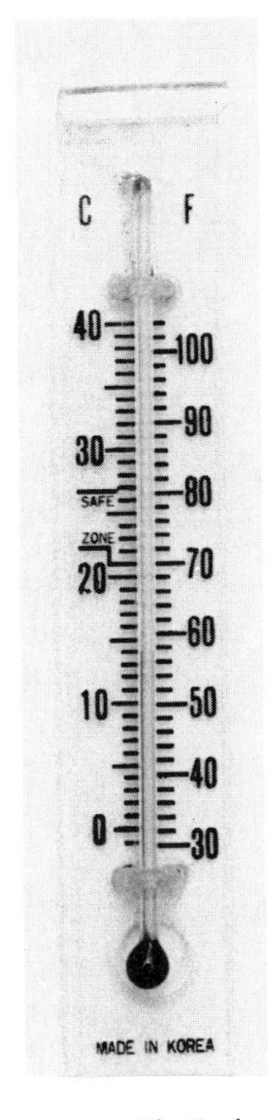

Figure 33 *Aquarium thermometer. The "safe zone" is the manufacturer's designation. Product endorsement is not implied.*

purchase test kits for determining these factors and have them ready.

ALKALINITY

In practical terms, *alkalinity* is a measure of the capacity of a volume of seawater or artificial seawater to weather the continuous input of acidic compounds without a rapid decline in pH. Acids are the natural products of many biological processes. Alkalinity controls pH, and its determination is a useful indicator of future pH status. Follow instructions included with the test kit (Figure 34). Determine alkalinity a day or two after the aquarium has been set up and everything is functioning (in other words, after the gravel and water have been added and the airlifts have been turned on). Prior soaking of the gravel in seawater or artificial seawater, as recommended in Procedure 5 (see Chapter 5), almost guarantees initial alkalinity values within the accceptable range of 2.5 to 3.0 milliequivalents per liter (mEq/L).[8] If the alkalinity requires adjustment, consult Chapter 10.

PH

A *pH test* is a determination of the acidity or basicity of the water. The waters of most marine aquariums range from pH 7.5 to 8.4. The acceptable range is 8.0 to 8.3; the ideal value is 8.2. Select a pH test kit designed for use with marine aquariums (Figure 35). *Test kits designed to determine pH in freshwater will give false readings.* Follow instructions included with the test kit, and determine the pH a day or two after the aquarium has been set up and everything is functioning (that is, after the gravel and water have been added and the airlifts have been turned on). Prior soaking of the gravel in seawater or artificial seawater, as recommended in Procedure 5 (see Chapter 5), helps keep initial pH values above 8.0. *Heavy, continuous aeration by airlift pumping, which drives off excess*

[8]An *equivalent*, Eq, is the amount of an ion required to equal the charge (positive or negative) of a mole of an ion with a single charge. For sodium, Na^{+}, which has only one (positive) charge, the number of equivalents equals the number of moles; for an ion with two charges (for example, carbonate, CO_3^{2-}), one mole equals two equivalents. A *milliequivalent* is 1/1000th of an equivalent. A *mole* is the quantity of a substance that has a weight in grams (properly, a mass in grams) numerically equal to its molecular weight. The *mass* of an object is the quantity of matter it contains; the *weight* of the same object is a measure of the force of gravity on it. A man weighing 150 pounds on Earth would weigh only 30 pounds on the moon, where gravity is less. His mass would be the same on both planets.

Figure 34 *Representative test kit for determining alkalinity. Product endorsement is not implied.* Source: Aquarium Systems, 8141 Tyler Boulevard, Mentor OH 44060.

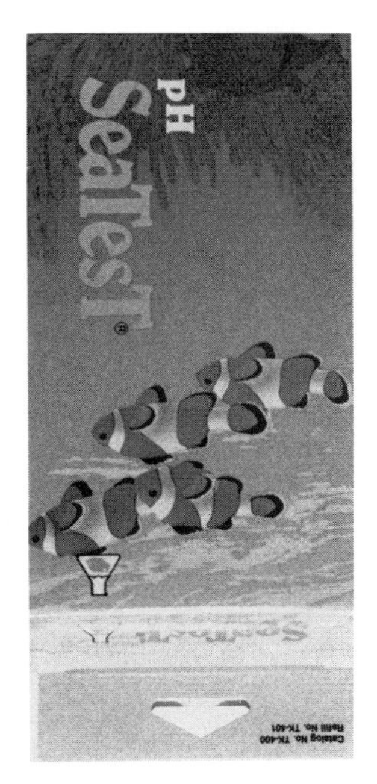

Figure 35 *Representative pH test kit for seawater and artificial seawater. Product endorsement is not implied.* Source: Aquarium Systems, 8141 Tyler Boulevard, Mentor OH 44060.

carbon dioxide, is the most effective means of sustaining pH values above 8.0. The importance of good air flow cannot be emphasized too strongly. As illustrated in Figure 28, the reaction of carbon dioxide with water produces carbonic acid, which reduces pH by making the water more acidic. If the pH requires adjustment, consult Chapter 10.

SPECIFIC GRAVITY

In simplified terms, *specific gravity* is the ratio of the density of seawater or artificial seawater to the density of pure water. Specific gravity increases as freshwater evaporates from an aquarium; it decreases if too much freshwater is then added to restore the original value (see below). During evaporation, freshwater is lost from an aquarium; most of the other components remain behind, rendering the solution "saltier." As defined previously, the density of a substance is its weight per volume. The density of pure water is 1.000 grams per cubic centimeter (g/cm^3). Seawater is approximately 2.5% denser than pure water, or 1.025 g/cm^3 compared with 1.000 g/cm^3. Specific gravity is a dimensionless ratio (it has no units of expression) because the units of the numerator and denominator cancel out, as shown by:

$$\frac{1.025\,\cancel{g}/\cancel{cm}^3}{1.000\,\cancel{g}/\cancel{cm}^3} = 1.025$$

Hydrometers (Figure 36), the instruments used to determine specific gravity, are calibrated at the factory against pure water. When a hydrometer is immersed in still seawater and stops bobbing, the value on its stem at the *miniscus* (the curved upper edge of the liquid where it meets the stem, Figure 36a) is the *hydrometer reading*. For maximum accuracy this value should be corrected for any difference between the temperature of the aquarium water and the temperature at which the hydrometer was calibrated by using correction tables or equations. Only the corrected value can properly be called *specific gravity.* However, most marine aquariums are maintained within a relatively narrow temperature range. For purposes here, a hydrometer reading serves as a practical measure of the specific gravity. In any case, minor variations in specific gravity readings caused by temperature discrepancies will not affect captive animals and plants adversely. *Marine aquarium waters should have specific gravity values within the range 1.023 to 1.025 at 80°F.*

Modern aquarium books sometimes recommend keeping the specific gravity at 1.022 or lower on the assumption that such environments are less stressful, particularly to fishes. This has no factual basis (see Chapter 15, Myth 8). The energy expended by marine fishes to maintain a proper balance of water and ions in their tissues is small compared with the amounts needed for digestion and many other physiological processes. If the specific gravity requires adjustment, consult Chapter 10.

According to some authors, specific gravity is an inferior, even amateurish, determination. In their view, salinity, conductivity, and refractive index are superior analytical determinants. I shall not describe these other methods because their utility in marine aquarium keeping is dubious. However, touting any method as superior to another is misleading, unless the reasons for its application are different or additional information can be revealed. In the operation of a marine aquarium, the objective is to gain a reproducible measure of the water's "saltiness" for purposes of maintaining the environment in a stable condition. Consequently, specific gravity is an adequate determinant.

The analytical determination of true *salinity*[9] is complex, and a salinity test kit does not exist. The practice of converting specific gravity values to units of salinity is acceptable, provided that *salinity* refers only to the simplified definition (see text footnote 9) and the test solution is seawater. Salinity is a meaningless term when used in reference to artificial seawaters.[10] In any case, the converted values yield no additional information, and the exercise is pointless.

Procedure 7 *How to Measure Specific Gravity Using Conventional Hydrometers*

1 Wash the hydrometer in tap water to remove salts, then wipe it dry.
2 Shut off all air to the aquarium and wait until the surface becomes still.

[9]The simplified definition of *salinity* is the total mass of substances dissolved in one kilogram (1 kg) of seawater. Analytically, *salinity* is the total mass in grams of all dissolved substances in 1 kg of seawater after all carbonate has been converted to oxide, all bromine and iodine replaced by chlorine, and all organic matter oxidized at 480°C. One kilogram = 1000 grams.

[10]In chemical oceanography, salinity determinations assume a specific set of conditions, one being that the water undergoing analysis is seawater and nothing else. Artificial seawaters differ in composition from seawater, and the discrepancies are not trivial. For a detailed discussion see Bidwell and Spotte (1985) in Additional Reading ("Advanced Aquarists" section).

3 Immerse the hydrometer slowly, push it gently under the surface, and let it float freely.
4 Examine the hydrometer for attached air bubbles and knock them off. After the instrument has come to rest, read the scale at the meniscus (Figure 36a).
5 Record the value in a notebook; also record the date.
6 Remove the hydrometer, rinse it with tap water, wipe it clean with a paper towel, and turn on the air.

Procedure 8 ***How to Measure Specific Gravity Using the SeaTest™ Hydrometer***

1 Rinse out the instrument (Figure 36b) with tap water to remove any residual salts.
2 Fill and empty the instrument once with aquarium water.
3 Fill to the mark with aquarium water. Examine the float for attached air bubbles and knock them off with a pencil.
4 Record the value and date in a notebook.
5 Pour the water back into the aquarium, rinse the instrument with tap water, and turn it upside down on a paper towel to dry.

TEMPERATURE CONTROL

For conventional marine aquariums, *temperature control* refers to raising the water temperature to a predetermined value and keeping it constant. Animals and plants indigenous to tropical and subtropical seas do well in environments maintained at 77 to 84°F with 80°F considered ideal. Species from temperate waters often require no heat at all, provided the room temperature does not fluctuate excessively.

All three types of aquariums (exhibit, quarantine, and treatment) require temperature control; therefore, all must have *immersion heaters* with thermostats (Figure 37). Immersion heaters are manufactured in several sizes of designated wattage. *A general guideline is 2 watts/gal of aquarium water if the room temperature is always 70°F or warmer, and 4 watts/gal if the room is cooler than 70°F for several hours each day.* For example, a 50-gal aquarium would need 100 or 200 watts, depending on whether the room was warm or cool. *Do not plug an immersion heater in without submerging it to the proper depth; otherwise the heater's glass case might crack. An immersion heater also cracks if removed from the water without being unplugged first and allowed to cool for 5 minutes while still sub-*

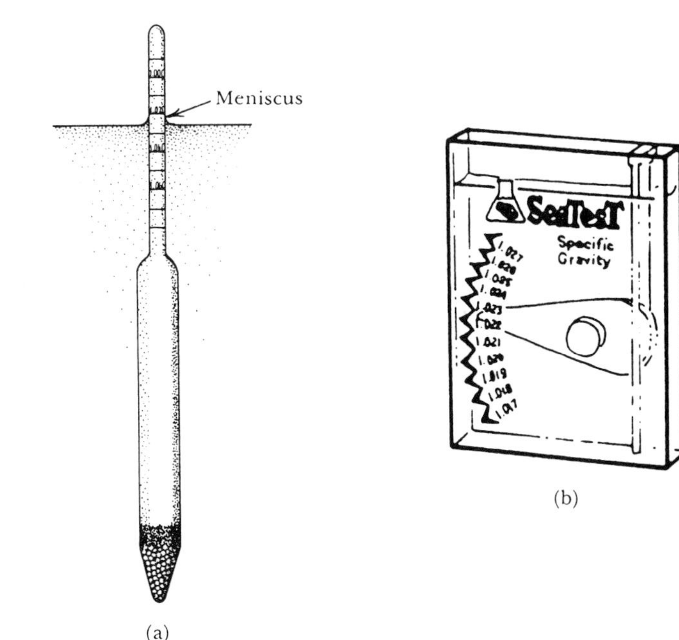

Figure 36 (a) *Conventional hydrometer. Read and record the value at the meniscus.* (b) *SeaTest™ Hydrometer. Before reading, tap the float with a pencil to dislodge any air bubbles. Product endorsement is not implied.* Sources: (a) S. Spotte, *Marine Aquarium Keeping: The Science, Animals, and Art,* John Wiley & Sons, Inc., © 1973, reprinted with permission. (b) Aquarium Systems, 8141 Tyler Boulevard, Mentor OH 44060.

merged. In both situations heating is uneven, and the section of the heater exposed to air becomes disproportionately hotter. The temperature differential between exposed and submerged sections stresses the glass case and causes cracking.

The performance of an immersion heater is seldom reflected accurately by its temperature scale (the temperature at which the thermostat is set), and some adjustment is usually required to stabilize the temperature. *It is safer to use two or more smaller immersion heaters than a single large one. This provides a safety factor if a heater malfunctions.*

CONDITIONING THE SUBGRAVEL FILTERS

Even if heterotrophic and nitrifying bacteria are present initially in the subgravel filters of the quarantine and exhibit aquariums, their numbers are too small to convert the amounts of organic

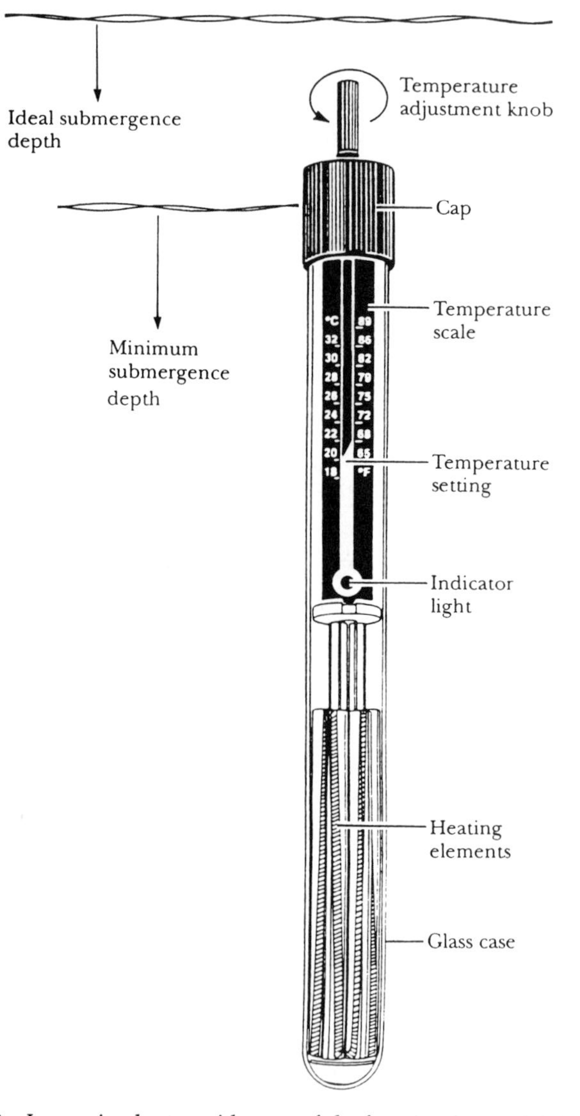

Figure 37 *Immersion heater with most of the functional parts labeled. Keep the heater submerged completely at all times to prevent the glass case from cracking. Unplug immersion heaters and let cool for 5 minutes before removing from an aquarium or exposing to the air during partial water changes. During operation, be sure the tip of the temperature adjustment knob is completely submerged. Product endorsement is not implied.* Source: Aquarium Systems, 8141 Tyler Boulevard, Mentor OH 44060; labeled by Stephen Spotte.

matter and inorganic nitrogen generated routinely by a healthy population of animals. The filtrants of both aquariums need to be aged or *conditioned* before animals and plants can be added. The filter bacteria must be allowed time to form slime layers on the gravel and reproduce. In a *conditioned subgravel filter,* first ammonia and then nitrite have reached their maximum concentrations (that is, they have peaked) and begun to decline (Figure 38). A subgravel filter is considered fully conditioned when the nitrite concentration has declined to almost zero. At temperatures above 70°F, this occurs in 2 months or less. The function of a conditioned subgravel filter is to (*1*) convert organic matter and inorganic nitrogen generated by the animals, plants, and bacteria to less objectionable chemical forms; and (*2*) maintain ammonia at concentrations too small to be determined with test kits. The conditioning process is lengthy, but critical. *You must resist every temptation to acquire specimens before the conditioning period is over.* To succumb is foolish. A predictable result will be the deaths of all new animals. If any survive they are likely to sicken and die later.

Conditioning involves adding small amounts of organic matter once at the beginning and small quantities of ammonia at regular intervals until the ammonia and nitrite concentrations peak and start to decline. Organic matter allows heterotrophic bacteria to accumulate. There is no convenient method of determining

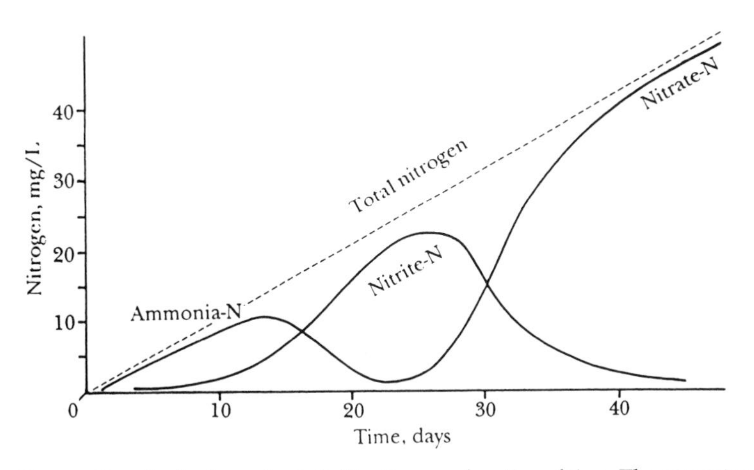

Figure 38 *Stylized graph of nitrification as a function of time. The concentration of ammonia peaks first, followed by the concentration of nitrite. Nitrate continues to increase, but the concentration can be controlled by regular partial water changes.* Source: Gary Adams, Department of Chemical Engineering Technology, Three Rivers Community College, Norwich, Connecticut.

the concentration of dissolved organic carbon in water. Ammonia provides an energy source that encourages nitrite formers to become established. The nitrite that is produced supplies energy for nitrate formers, which take over the next step of the nitrification conversion sequence.

Organic matter can be added in the form of a small piece of cooked fish or shrimp. Ammonia is supplied conveniently as an *ammonium salt* (for example, ammonium chloride or ammonium sulfate), either dry or in premixed solutions (Figure 39). After the aquarium has become conditioned, the remaining pieces of fish or shrimp can be removed and replaced with living animals. From then on all bacterial processes should continue uninterrupted, sustained by waste products (mainly organic matter and ammonia) generated naturally.

Heterotrophic and nitrifying bacteria appear quickly in aquariums. However, the conditioning process can be accelerated by adding a handful of old gravel from the subgravel filter of an established aquarium. Some authors recommend "seeding" the new subgravel filter at home with gravel from a dealer's aquarium. This dangerous practice should be avoided. Hundreds of

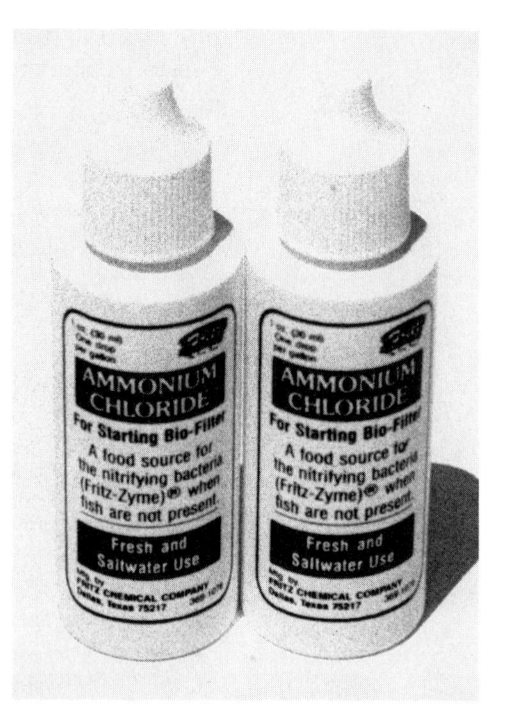

Figure 39 *Premixed ammonium chloride solution. The same supplier also sells ammonium chloride salt. Available from Fritz Aquaculture, P.O. Drawer 17040, Dallas TX 75217. Product endorsement is not implied.*

fishes and invertebrates pass routinely through a dealer's aquariums. Many of these animals arrive carrying infectious diseases; others contract them on the premises. Infectious organisms can often be isolated from aquarium environments, including the gravel and water, which is ample proof of their presence.

Another popular technique is to purchase packages of freeze-dried nitrifiers or similar products and add the contents to a new aquarium (Figure 40). This practice, although not dangerous, is unnecessary and often ineffective. Still other products purport to circumvent the conditioning process: ammonia, nitrite, nitrate, and phosphate are removed without effort by purely chemical means. The high ammonia concentrations so typical of new aquariums are thus avoided simply by adding some crystals or a liquid straight from a container. Even if such claims are true, supplanting essential biological processes merely delays conditioning of the subgravel filter, which relies on the presence of ammonia, nitrite, and other compounds to encourage an adequate population of filter bacteria. The subgravel filter cannot become conditioned if the nutrients have been removed, because a natural and effective population of bacteria will fail to

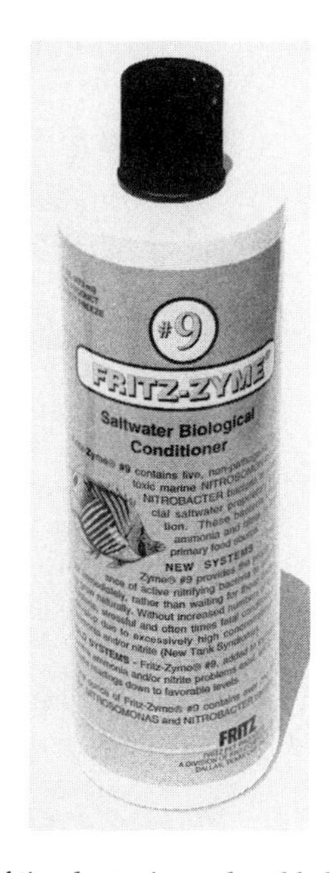

Figure 40 *Packaged nitrifying bacteria can be added to new marine aquariums to shorten the conditioning period, but the results are sometimes disappointing. Many packaged products have been freeze-dried; in the product illustrated here, the bacteria have been suspended in a nutrient solution. Available from Fritz Aquaculture, P.O. Drawer 17040, Dallas TX 75217. Product endorsement is not implied.*

develop. Ignore the advertisements; natural seeding in combination with your patience is the only method needed.

Procedure 9 describes how to monitor the conditioning process by measuring the sequential rise and fall of the different forms of nitrogen. *Notice that only the nitrogen component of ammonia, nitrite, and nitrate is typically expressed in concentrations; to emphasize this we label it with "N" (for example, ammonia-N). Notice also that units of concentration are milligrams per liter (mg/L),*[11] *not parts per million (ppm) as stated incorrectly in the literature included with some test kits.*[12] A value of 2, for example, should be expressed as 2 mg/L ammonia-N, not as "2 ppm ammonia." The assumption is that the tiny sample of water used in the analysis is representative of all the water in the aquarium (in other words, that every liter has 2 mg of ammonia-N). A gallon of water is equivalent to 3.785 L.

Nitrite and nitrate are less toxic than ammonia and therefore less important. Nonetheless, they provide insight into the status of the conditioning process and should be determined every third day for the first two months. Values of 10 and 25 for nitrite and nitrate, respectively, would be recorded as 10 mg/L nitrite-N and 25 mg/L nitrate-N.[13]

[11]1 gram (g) = 1000 milligrams (mg); 1 liter (L) = 1000 milliliters (mL).

[12]In proper chemical usage, *parts per million*, ppm, means milligrams per kilogram of solution (that is, milligrams of the substance being determined per kilogram of seawater or artificial seawater). The relationship is one of mass per mass (see text footnote 8 for the definition of mass). However, no water is ever weighed during a test kit analysis. Instead, the reagents are added to a specific volume of aquarium water that has been removed for testing. Results are then expressed in terms of the mass of test substance (for example, ammonia-N or nitrite-N) found to be present *per volume* of water in the aquarium; in other words, in units of mg/L, not mg/kg. This mass per volume ratio is not the equivalent of parts per million except when the water being tested is pure water at 4°C. At this temperature, pure water has a theoretical density of 1.000 g/cm^3. Only under these restricted conditions does 1 L of water have a mass of 1 kg.

[13]Some test kits express ammonia, nitrite, and nitrate in ionic form; in other words, as NH_4^+, NO_2^-, and NO_3^-, not in terms of the nitrogen component. To conform with standard usage, the results obtained with these kits should be converted to milligrams per liter of ammonia-N, nitrite-N, and nitrate-N. Atomic weights of the elements nitrogen, hydrogen, and oxygen are, respectively, 14, 1, and 16. Ammonium ion has one atom of nitrogen and four of hydrogen for a molecular weight of 18. To obtain the approximate concentration of ammonia-N, find the ratio of the molecular weight of ammonium ion to the atomic weight of nitrogen (18/14). Afterward, divide the test kit result by the quotient, which is 1.3. Nitrite ion has two atoms of oxygen and one of nitrogen for a molecular weight of 46. Nitrate ion has an additional oxygen atom, and its molecular weight is 62. To obtain the approximate concentration of nitrite-N, find the ratio of the molecular weight of nitrite ion to the atomic weight of nitrogen (46/14), then divide the test kit result by the quotient, which is 3.3. To obtain the approximate nitrate-N concentration, divide the test kit result by the quotient 4.4 (that is, 62/14).

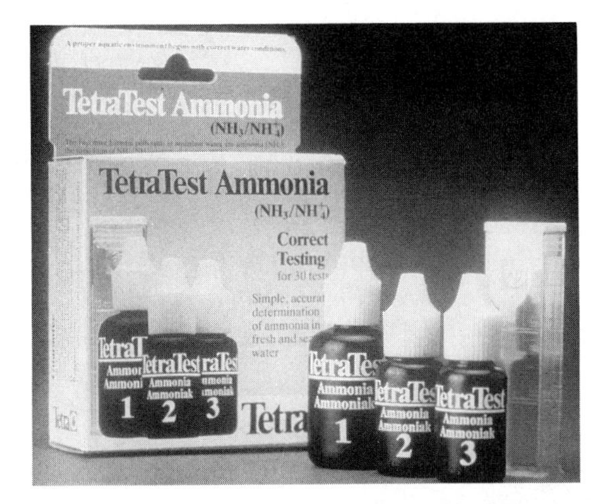

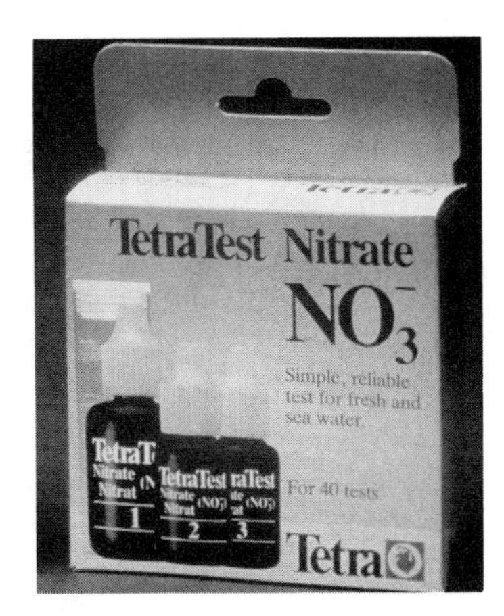

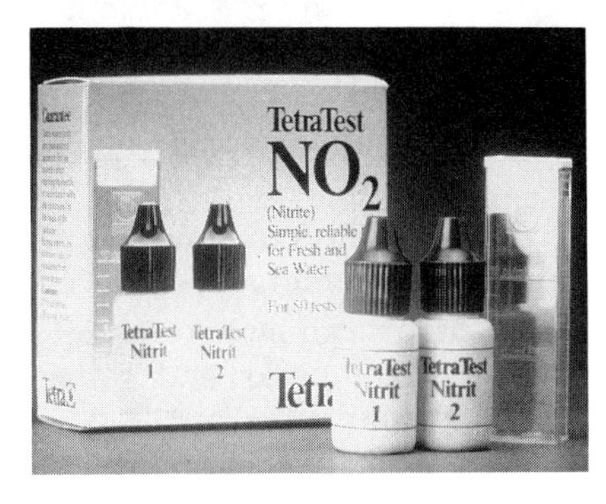

(a)

(b)

Figure 41 *Representative test kits for determining inorganic nitrogen as ammonia, nitrite, and nitrate. Product endorsement is not implied.* Sources: (a) Tetra Sales (U.S.A.), 201 Tabor Road, Morris Plains NJ 07950; (b) Aquarium Systems, 8141 Tyler Boulevard, Mentor OH 44060.

Procedure 9 *How to Condition a New Subgravel Filter*

1 Do not start until the exhibit and quarantine aquariums are fully operational. Final adjustments in water temperature to attain 80°F can be made during the conditioning period.
2 Add a thumbnail-sized piece of cooked fish or shrimp for each 30 gal of water. Do not repeat.
3 Add a pinch of an ammonium salt (ammonium chloride or ammonium sulfate) for each 30 gal of water. If a solution of an ammonium salt is purchased instead, add the specified number of drops per gallon of aquarium water.
4 Determine the ammonia concentration at least every third day with the ammonia test kit (Figure 41). Record the concentration and date of the analysis after each determination in milligrams per liter of ammonia-N.
5 Starting on day 8, also determine nitrite and nitrate. Record the concentrations and date of the analyses after each determination in milligrams per liter of nitrite-N and nitrate-N.
6 Repeat ammonia additions every other day until the concentration peaks and starts to decline (see Figure 38). This should occur within 3 weeks at temperatures of 70°F and warmer. Nitrification is slower in cold waters.
7 After the ammonia concentration peaks, remove any remaining pieces of fish or shrimp and discard them.
8 The quarantine aquarium is now ready to receive animals. However, conditioning is not complete until nitrite peaks and then nearly disappears (see Figure 38).
9 Leave the exhibit aquarium empty of animals and plants but fully functioning for another 3 weeks while the first group of animals is brought through quarantine. During this time the filter bacteria in the exhibit aquarium will remain viable. To sustain their capacity to form nitrite, add a pinch of ammonium salt for each 30 gal once a week for the next 2 weeks. Alternatively, add the specified number of drops of ammonium salt solution per gallon of aquarium water.

CHAPTER

7 The Quarantine Period

Synopsis *Never add animals that have not been quarantined to the exhibit aquarium. The recommended minimum quarantine period is 3 weeks. Plan on adding no more than 1 linear inch of animal for every 6 gal of water. A quarantrine aquarium holds less than its stated volume because some of the space has been taken up by the subgravel filter and flower pots. Moreover, an aquarium is never filled to the top. If instructions in Chapter 3 have been followed, you know how much water has been added.*

The quarantine aquarium is now ready to receive animals. I consider your effort in preparation to have been eminently worthwhile, although some authors would disagree. They recommend buying the animals all at once and adding them simultaneously to the exhibit aquarium on the assumption that each individual has the opportunity to establish its own living space before a few members of the group can become dominant. This argument, which considers only the social consequences of community aquarium living (see Chapter 13), is flawed in two respects. First, if the aquarium has been decorated correctly, spaces for later arrivals will be available (see Chapter 9). Second, there are potentially harmful physiological and health effects caused by suddenly introducing too many animals at once. These effects become especially pertinent when the aquarium is new.

A newly conditioned subgravel filter is fragile, not yet in balance with the waste load it will eventually receive. Secondary peaks in the ammonia concentration often appear when the capacity of a new subgravel filter has been exceeded. Not uncommonly, toxic levels of ammonia persist for several days while the filter bacteria adjust. Such conditions are stressful to the animals.

Diseases appear with alarming frequency in new aquariums, because the number of animals (or their sizes) exceeds both the subgravel filter capacity and the volume of the aquarium. *Aquarists who add new animals directly to the exhibit aquarium risk losing these and all later additions if just one specimen carries an infectious disease.* Once established, infectious disease organisms can become so pervasive that complete sterilization of the water, gravel, decorations, and fixtures is the only remedy (see Chapter 12). The treated water will then have to be discarded, new water added, and the subgravel filter conditioned again. Persistent disease problems are discouraging. A less impetuous approach based on rigorous quarantine procedures yields better results.

Never add animals that have not been quarantined to the exhibit aquarium. The recommended minimum quarantine period is 3 weeks. Obviously, all the animals cannot be purchased at once if the quarantine aquarium is substantially smaller than the exhibit aquarium. If the volume is only 20 gal, not more than one or two specimens at a time can be maintained safely for 3 weeks.

Figure 42 *Flower pots can serve as hiding places in quarantine aquariums. The pots shown are terra cotta; plastic pots are preferable because their surfaces are easier to clean.* Source: Modified from S. Spotte, *Marine Aquarium Keeping: The Science, Animals, and Art,* John Wiley & Sons, Inc., © 1973, reprinted with permission.

Procedure 10 *How to Prepare to Quarantine New Animals*

1 Three weeks have passed. Be certain the subgravel filter of the quarantine aquarium has approached a conditioned state by once again determining the concentrations of ammonia, nitrite, and nitrate.

2 Determine alkalinity, pH, and specific gravity; adjust as necessary (see Chapter 10).

3 Arrange three or four small plastic flower pots on top of the gravel (Figure 42) to provide shelter spaces (see Chapter 9) for new animals.

4 *Plan on adding no more than 1 linear inch of animal for every 6 gal of water*. Keep in mind that a quarantine aquarium holds less than its stated volume because some of the space has been taken up by the subgravel filter and flower pots. Moreover, an aquarium is never filled to the top. If instructions in early paragraphs of Chapter 3 have been followed, you know how much water has been added.

C H A P T E R

8 Animal Selection

Synopsis *Five criteria are useful when selecting animals in a dealer's aquariums: (1) immediate condition, (2) potential survivorship, (3) ease of care, (4) compatibility with other animals, and (5) potential for growth. Healthy appearance does not guarantee survival, but the potentially reduced survivorship of animals that are obviously unhealthy is sufficient cause for rejection. Stock no more than 1 linear inch of animal for every 6 gal of water based on estimated lengths at or near adulthood, not necessarily at the time of acquisition. Understocking a new aquarium has two advantages. First, the possibility of ammonia toxicity is greatly diminished because the capacity of the subgravel filter is less likely to be exceeded. Second, future growth still allows adequate space for normal social interaction.*

Several criteria are useful when selecting animals for a marine aquarium. I offer five in decreasing order of importance: (*1*) immediate condition, (2) potential survivorship, (3) ease of care, (4) compatibility with other animals, and (5) potential for growth. Notice that attractiveness (for example, form, pattern, and coloration) is not included. Many of the prettiest animals in the sea are among the most difficult to keep alive in captivity. *As a beginning aquarist you must resist buying any animal based on the single criterion of attractiveness.*

IMMEDIATE CONDITION

The condition of the animals in a dealer's aquariums ranges from healthy to dead. Most fall somewhere between these extremes. Healthy appearance does not guarantee survival, but the potentially reduced survivorship of animals that are obviously unhealthy is sufficient cause for rejection.

Before buying an animal, examine it carefully for several minutes. A checklist of salient features is provided in Table 4. If the specimen you are evaluating is a fish, note the appearance of its skin, fins and fin rays, mouth, and eyes. *Fin rays* are the stiffening structures that support the fins. They can be soft and flexible or modified into bony spines. Injuries such as abrasions, torn fins, or broken fin rays, which are often caused by careless handling, can result in later manifestation of an infectious disease.

The skin of a healthy fish is shiny and bright because the mucous coating is completely transparent (not opaque) and therefore not obvious. Small (pinhead-sized) white spots and yellowish, velvety patches that impart a dull appearance are signs of diseases caused by *protozoans* (single-celled animals) and other microorganisms. Open red lesions are one sign of bacterial disease. Skin on the external surface of the mouth should be intact; the eyes should be clear and undamaged. The fins of a

TABLE 4 Criteria for acceptance or rejection of animals in a dealer's aquariums based on immediate condition.

Acceptance	Rejection
Fishes	
Skin unblemished, bright, and shiny	Skin with pinhead-sized white spots, dull with a yellow velvety appearance, or with lesions; mouth skin frayed
Mucous coating transparent and not obvious	Mucous coating opaque
Fins intact, fin rays straight and unbroken	Fins frayed, fin rays broken
Starvation not extreme	Belly hollow in torpedo-shaped fishes; in laterally compressed fishes, area above spinal column sunken and pinched (in extreme cases, also area below spinal column)
Activity normal for species	Activity lethargic for active species
Swimming motions normal	Swimming erratic and jerky
Breathing slow and regular	Breathing labored
Fins in normal positions	Fins folded
Winner of a territorial dispute	Loser of a territorial dispute
Invertebrates	
Crustaceans with all appendages intact	Crustaceans with eyes, legs, or antennae missing
Sea anemones with columns and tentacles extended fully	Sea anemones with columns and tentacles shriveled and collapsed
Sea urchins with spines erect	Sea urchins with drooping spines
Sea stars active	Sea stars inactive

healthy fish are intact, not ripped or frayed, and the fin rays are straight and unbroken.

Many dealers feed their animals intermittently or not at all, preferring instead to sell them quickly. The fishes and invertebrates you see in a dealer's aquariums might not have eaten since being captured in a remote region of the Indo-West Pacific or Caribbean. Depending on logistics of capture, transport, and distribution, some specimens will have been starved for 2 weeks or longer. Not surprisingly, animals held by dealers are sometimes thin, particularly species that lose body weight quickly. Starved specimens should be rejected because they might not recover.

In fishes the consequences of starvation take many forms, depending to some extent on body shape. Species tending naturally toward a rounded or torpedo shape have hollow bellies when starved. Fishes that are compressed laterally (flattened from side to side) lose weight between the spinal column and dorsal fin (Figure 43). This gives them a pinched appearance, as if they had been gripped just above the spinal column and squeezed. Drastically starved specimens of the laterally compressed form can also look pinched below the spinal column.

An animal's behavior is the last factor to evaluate. Most healthy fishes move about, although groupers and other species that hide are less active. A fish's swimming motions should be natural and fluid, not erratic and jerky. Look for individuals that seem to be searching for food by picking at the bottom and show similar signs of having adapted to captivity. Breathing should be

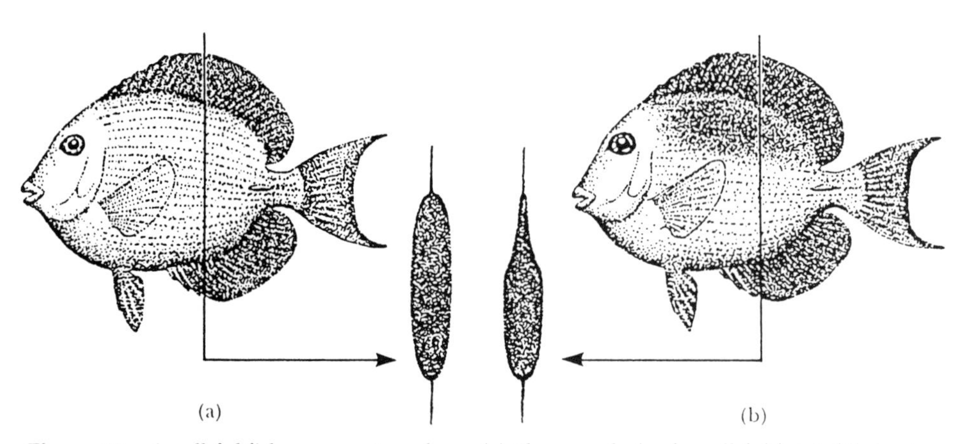

Figure 43 *A well-fed fish versus a starved one. (a) The upper body of a well-fed fish is filled out, as shown in this cross section. (b) A cross section of a starved fish illustrates how the upper body becomes emaciated even though the belly might be full.* Source: S. Spotte, *Marine Aquarium Keeping: The Science, Animals, and Art*, John Wiley & Sons, Inc., © 1973, reprinted with permission.

slow and regular; avoid specimens with labored breathing. The fins of healthy fishes are partly or fully erect. A fish that remains motionless with fins folded tightly against its body is often sick. Finally, notice any evidence of fighting. Timid specimens relegated to a corner by more aggressive aquarium-mates should not be selected. Choose the winner of a territorial dispute, not the loser.

Invertebrates can also show signs of distress. Before buying a shrimp or crab, be certain that its eyes, legs, and antennae are intact. The column and tentacles of a sea anemone should be extended fully, not shriveled and collapsed. A healthy sea urchin's spines normally are erect; those of a sick sea urchin droop. Healthy sea stars ordinarily are active.

SURVIVORSHIP

Survivorship is an organism's projected longevity (in other words, its probability of surviving) when known or suspected mitigating factors are considered within the context of average life span. *Probability* implies a statistical basis. Actuarial tables used by the insurance industry describe probabilities of human survivorship in statistical terms: the survivorship of smokers versus nonsmokers, persons whose families have histories of heart disease versus those whose families do not, and so forth. Actuarial tables for fishes and invertebrates do not exist, and survivorship is therefore unpredictable. We must rely on experience and intuition instead. The criteria discussed in the previous section are subjective assessments of *immediate survivorship*. However, long-term or *extended survivorship* is also worth considering.

Factors that influence extended survivorship of captive fishes and invertebrates are numerous and incompletely understood. They include chemical imbalances in the water, social factors, immediate previous history in captivity (starvation, exposure to infectious disease organisms), age, flexibility in acceptance and digestion of unfamiliar foods, and general condition at the time of acquisition.

A common mistake is to select animals—particularly fishes—with low probabilities of extended survivorship. Butterflyfishes and angelfishes are best avoided until the aquarium is well established and you have gained experience. Many species have specific food requirements. Such *feeding specialists* (see Chapter 11) will eventually starve to death in captivity. Examples are butterflyfishes and angelfishes that subsist exclusively on coral mucus or living sponges. These dietary items are impossible to provide in captivity, and suitable substitutes have not been discovered. Juveniles occasionally learn to accept less exotic foods and grow to adult size, but specimens acquired as adults seldom survive the transition.

Parrotfishes in nature eat algae growing on dead coral (Figure 44), but few species live for long even in algae-filled aquariums. Conversely, most tangs and surgeonfishes, many of which are algae eaters in the wild, adapt quickly to standard aquarium diets without ill effects. In some cases the selection of an especially voracious species jeopardizes the survival of smaller species (for example, blennies, damselfishes, and gobies) that do well otherwise. Groupers, scorpionfishes (including turkeyfishes), squirrelfishes, and some morays prey on other fishes small enough to swallow. These and other large predators are best avoided unless the other aquarium inhabitants are large. Schooling fishes are inherently social, and some species seem to survive longer if two or more are maintained together. This is a subjective assessment and has no scientific basis.

Crustaceans such as shrimps and crabs generally demonstrate excellent extended survivorship, as do sea urchins and many sea stars. Some species of sea anemones survive poorly unless kept under bright light. Live corals are not recommended for beginning aquarists, nor are mollusks (for example, snails and scallops). Most corals and marine mollusks require special care.

EASE OF CARE

Some species adapt easily to aquarium life, requiring little in terms of special care (Table 5). Animals in this category accept most foods readily and resist infectious diseases well. They tolerate intermittent periods of poor water quality and the occasional incident when a heater or air compressor malfunctions.

Most wrasses do well in aquariums, although species that spend the night buried in the gravel require loosely packed materials such as coral hash (see Chapter 13), and the depth of the filtrant should be at least 3 inches. As mentioned previously, many species of angelfishes and butterflyfishes fare poorly in captivity. If you attempt to keep them, remember that small specimens (juveniles) are more likely to survive than adults. Blennies and gobies are generally hardy. So are surgeonfishes and tangs, although they are among the first to show starvation effects in a dealer's aquariums. Newly acquired surgeonfishes and tangs sometimes feed poorly in the beginning, even after prolonged starvation. Inducing them to feed actively and regain lost body weight during the quarantine period is important. Afterward, extended survivorship is good, and most do not require special care.

Figure 44 *Scrape marks made by grazing parrotfishes. The teeth of parrotfishes are adapted for scraping algae off the surfaces of dead coral and coral rock. Photographed at Pine Cay, Turks and Caicos Islands, British West Indies, 22 feet.*

COMPATIBILITY WITH OTHER ANIMALS

It is important to select animals that are likely to coexist peacefully and be compatible with the other aquarium inhabitants. This is especially true of fishes. Aggression, if expressed at all, should be limited to brief chases, never extended attacks that inflict injury. The term *compatibility* is *always* relative. Not surpris-

TABLE 5 Groups of marine aquarium fishes and invertebrates in the ease-of-care category.

Fishes	
Basslets	Roundheads
Blennies	Scorpionfishes
Damselfishes	Sea basses
Drums	Squirrelfishes
Eeltail catfishes	Surgeonfishes and tangs
Filefishes	Triggerfishes
Gobies	Wrasses
Hawkfishes	
Invertebrates	
Crustaceans (crabs and shrimps)	
Sea urchins	

TABLE 6 Compatibility of common groups of fishes and invertebrates in community marine aquariums.

	Animal Group	Sometimes Incompatible With the Following Animal Groups
	Fishes	
1	Angelfishes	1, 16, 27
2	Angelfishes (pygmy)	2
3	Basslets	17–19, 21, 23
4	Blennies	17–19, 21, 23
5	Butterflyfishes	5
6	Cardinalfishes	17–19, 21, 23
7	Damselfishes[1]	17–19, 21, 23
8	Dottybacks	17–19, 21, 23
9	Dragonettes	17–19, 21, 23
10	Drums	17–19, 21, 23, 27
11	Eeltail catfishes	—
12	Filefishes	27, 30
13	Gobies	17–19, 21, 23
14	Hawkfishes	17–19, 21, 23
15	Jawfishes	17–19, 21, 23
16	Moorish idol	1
17	Morays	3, 4, 6–10, 13–15, 26, 27
18	Roundheads	3, 4, 6–10, 13–15, 26, 27
19	Scorpionfishes	3, 4, 6–10, 13–15, 26, 27
20	Sea basses (anthiines, others)	—
21	Sea basses (groupers)	3, 4, 6–10, 13–15, 26, 27
22	Seahorses	17–19, 21, 23
23	Squirrelfishes	3, 4, 6–10, 13–15, 26, 27
24	Surgeonfishes and tangs	27
25	Triggerfishes	27, 30
26	Wrasses (small species)	3, 4, 6–10, 13–15, 26, 27
	Invertebrates	
27	Crustaceans (crabs and shrimps)	1, 10, 12, 17, 18, 20, 22–25
28	Sea Anemones	—
29	Sea stars	—
30	Sea urchins	12, 25

[1]Anemonefishes (which are damselfishes) are usually peaceful despite being territorial (see Chapter 13).

ingly, compatibility between species—and among individuals of the same species—is largely unpredictable. For example, two individuals might be compatible if they differ substantially in size. Under different circumstances the same individuals might get along only if their sizes are similar.

Intraspecific aggression is directed against members of the same species; *interspecific aggression* is displayed against individuals of other species. In cases of intraspecific aggression, the compatibility problem can be solved simply by keeping only one individual of the species. This rule applies especially to certain angelfishes and damselfishes (Table 6). Sometimes two or more individuals can be kept together if they are small, the aquarium is large, and adequate shelter spaces are available (see Chapter 9). Interspecific aggression is more difficult to predict and control. Neither form of aggression is inherently dangerous unless space is restricted. Some chasing is natural and therefore inevitable, but watch for signs of overt aggression. These include relentless chasing and damage to the fins and scales of less dominant individuals.

TABLE 7 Approximate length at maturity of some groups of common marine aquarium fishes.[1]

Fishes	Approximate Length,[2] inches
Angelfishes	18
Angelfishes (pygmy)	8
Basslets	5
Blennies	6
Butterflyfishes	9
Cardinalfishes	7
Damselfishes	7
Dottybacks	5
Dragonettes	7
Drums	9
Eeltail catfishes	6
Filefishes	18
Gobies	6
Hawkfishes	10
Jawfishes	6
Moorish idol	9
Morays	40
Roundheads	6
Scorpionfishes	14
Sea basses (anthiines, others)	10
Sea basses (groupers)	24
Seahorses	6
Squirrelfishes	12
Surgeonfishes and tangs	18
Triggerfishes	23
Wrasses	12

[1]For particular species, consult Additional Reading ("Identification Guides" section), especially Burgess et al. (1988) and Randall (1983b).

[2]Actual length attained is species dependent. Tabular values assume that only smaller species are kept.

POTENTIAL FOR GROWTH

Aquarium animals grow, and many species have the potential to outgrow most home aquariums. The physiological and social effects of excessive growth are the same as overstocking with too many animals. The term used in both situations is *crowding* (the term *overcrowding* is redundant). Physiologically, the animals can produce more waste products than the subgravel filter is able to accommodate, culminating in a deteriorating environment. Crowding also has social implications if the animals outgrow their shelter places. With no place to hide, timid specimens can be harassed unmercifully by more aggressive members of their own and other species.

Stock no more than 1 linear inch of animal for every 6 gal of water based on estimated lengths at or near adulthood, not necessarily at the time of acquisition. For example, a juvenile damselfish that is less than 1 inch long might grow to 2 inches in 6 months. If you select such a fish, think of it as being 2 inches long.

Understocking a new aquarium has two advantages. First, the possibility of ammonia toxicity is greatly diminished because the capacity of the subgravel filter is less likely to be exceeded. Second, future growth still allows adequate space for normal social interaction. Table 7 lists projected lengths of a few groups of commonly available fishes.

CHAPTER

9 Decorating

Synopsis *Marine aquarium decorations make attractive settings; more important is their function as shelter spaces for the inhabitants. Decide on the theme of the exhibit aquarium and choose appropriate decorations (for example, corals for coral reef displays). Bleached corals (corals that were previously alive) look unnatural, encourage destruction of coral reefs, and are usually devoid of proper shelter spaces. Plastic decorations are preferable. Make holes in them on one side to provide access for aquarium animals. Place the unmarred sides toward the front glass. Arrange decorations so that the holes are accessible and swimming patterns of the fishes are not interrupted. When turning out the room lights, dim them gradually over 10 minutes. This allows the inhabitants time to locate their shelter spaces and settle down for the night.*

Aquarium decorations serve two functions. First, they make an attractive setting, perhaps reminiscent of a coral reef or rocky shore. Decorating an aquarium by selecting and placing the pieces of décor is an act of artistic expression. Second—and more important—decorations provide appropriate living spaces for the aquarium's inhabitants. Nature once provided food and shelter for the fishes and invertebrates in your care. As an aquarist, this is now your responsibility.

Coral reefs, rocky reefs, and similar habitats are riddled with labyrinthine passages, nearly all of them occupied by fishes and invertebrates. Coral reefs in particular provide an endless variety of *shelter spaces* (Figure 45). For animals that are active during the day, a proper shelter offers a safe resting place at night. Nocturnal animals emerge from their shelters at dusk and return to them at dawn. Most inhabitants of coral and rocky reefs use the same shelters throughout their lives. The availability of adequate, permanent shelter spaces has a subtle but enormously important effect on the survivorship of aquarium animals.

Figure 45 *Coral reefs provide uncountable numbers of shelter spaces for fishes and invertebrates. Photographed at Bonaire, Netherlands Antilles, 65 feet.*

SHAPES OF DECORATIONS

Before acquiring any decorations, decide on the theme or motif of the exhibit aquarium (for example, coral reef or rocky reef). The theme determines which kinds of decorations are appropriate. For example, pieces of coral would look out of place in a display of coastal New England fishes and invertebrates.

After choosing a theme, decide on the approximate number of specimens you intend to keep (see Chapter 8). Each animal needs a shelter space to which it can retire in solitude or hide if chased. Shelter spaces for small fishes, shrimps, and crabs should have openings large enough to be entered but too small for larger animals. Ordinarily, aquarium decorations require some modification. Avoid bleached corals (corals that were previously alive). They look unnatural (living corals are colorful), and by purchasing them you encourage further collections, which are damaging to living reefs. Moreover, the bleached corals sold by dealers seldom provide adequate shelter for any animals except shrimps and crabs, which are able to squeeze into small crevices.

Corals made of plastic simulate nature but spare coral reefs. Some manufactured products are solid throughout and devoid of shelter spaces. However, plastic decorations that are hollow can be modified easily with a hacksaw or by breaking off the edges with your fingers. Select several pieces and make holes in them on one side (Figure 46). The unmarred sides can be placed so that they face the front of the aquarium. A plastic coral so modified is still decorative while serving its function as a shelter space (Figure 47).

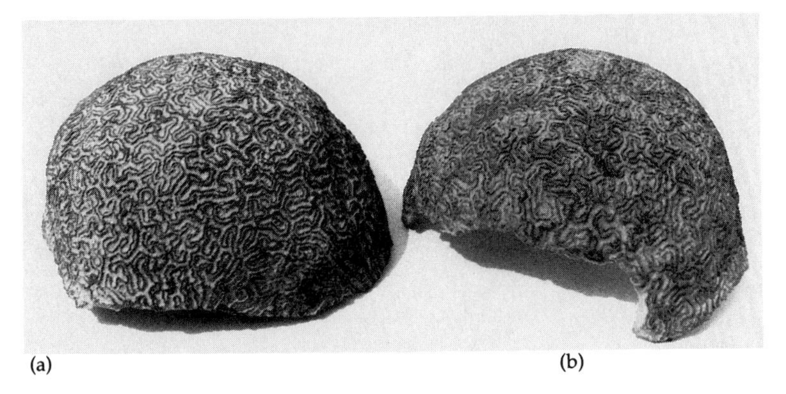
(a) (b)

Figure 46 *Plastic corals ordinarily require modification to provide shelter spaces for aquarium animals.* (a) *Plastic brain coral as manufactured.* (b) *Plastic brain coral after some of the edges have been broken off so that large fishes can get inside.*

(a)

(b)

Figure 47 *Emperor angelfish* (a) *leaving and* (b) *entering its personal shelter space underneath a modified plastic brain coral. Notice that the coral has two openings to allow access from different directions.*

PLACEMENT OF DECORATIONS

Arrange decorations with enough space among them for animals to use the openings. Push them into the gravel, although not so deeply as to bury the holes and block access. Place taller pieces toward the back of the aquarium, where they do not interrupt the swimming patterns of fishes, and leave some open space near the center for small schooling fishes. After a day or two, every animal will have staked out a shelter space, and when the room lights are dimmed at the end of the day, all inhabitants will suddenly disappear from view. *When turning out the room lights, dim them gradually over 10 minutes. This allows the inhabitants time to locate their shelter spaces and settle down for the night.*

CHAPTER

10 Maintenance

Synopsis *Routine maintenance is the most important aspect of marine aquarium keeping. The exhibit and quarantine aquariums should be cleaned at least every 2 weeks and more often if necessary. Regular cleaning, along with regular partial water changes, keeps the environment in a stable condition and eliminates most of the need to make adjustments in specific gravity, alkalinity, and pH. Discard at least 25% of the water and replace it with new seawater or artificial seawater every time the aquarium is cleaned. Replacing some of the water regularly lowers the nitrate concentration, removes some of the dissolved organic carbon (including a portion of the greenish-yellow pigment), restores alkalinity, and keeps pH and specific gravity within recommended ranges. The pH is kept in adjustment partly by continuous, vigorous aeration from airlift pumping, which drives off excess carbon dioxide. However, addition or subtraction of carbon dioxide has no effect on alkalinity. Consequently, neither does aeration. Without vigorous aeration, a situation can develop in which alkalinity is within the acceptable range of 2.5 to 3.0 mEq/L but the pH declines to below 8.0. Airlift performance is important in pH control. At maximum capacity, filtered water emerges from an airlift in a strong, smooth stream. Spurting water indicates reduced capacity caused by excessive air flow or a low water level in the aquarium. The pH of seawater or artificial seawater in marine aquariums declines by 0.1 unit or less each week. When necessary, adjust the pH upward to 8.2 with baking soda (sodium bicarbonate), which simultaneously restores alkalinity. Keep the specific gravity between 1.023 and 1.025 at 80°F by adding small amounts of dechlorinated tap water to compensate for evaporation. To help prevent the transmission of infectious diseases, always use dedicated equipment (siphon hoses, buckets, and other utensils used only with a specific aquarium).*

Routine maintenance is the most important aspect of marine aquarium keeping. Aquariums get dirty and must be cleaned regularly. Silty *detritus* (also called *aquarium dust*, or *mulm*) accumulates in the gravel, interrupting water flow through the subgravel filter and adding to the organic loading. The water turns greenish yellow, and the glass, decorations, and airlifts become coated with algae and biological slime. A dirty aquarium is unsightly and vaguely unhealthy in appearance; it also signals deterioration of the environment. The exhibit and quarantine aquariums should be cleaned a minimum of every 2 weeks and more often if necessary. *Regular cleaning, along with regular partial water changes, maintains the environment in a stable condition and eliminates most of the need to make adjustments in specific gravity, alkalinity, and pH.*

A partial water change should be part of any effort to clean an aquarium. Discard at least 25% of the water and replace the volume discarded with new seawater or artificial seawater every time the aquarium is cleaned. *Replacing some of the water regularly lowers the nitrate concentration, removes some of the dissolved organic carbon (including a portion of the greenish-yellow pigment), restores alkalinity, and keeps pH and specific gravity within recommended ranges.* Some authors see little need for partial water changes, although I disagree. In human terms, subjecting aquarium animals to a tired, dirty environment is like shutting yourself inside a crowded room filled with cooking odors and cigar smoke. Given a choice, most of us would open the windows and replace part of the air.

To help prevent the transmission of infectious diseases, always use *dedicated equipment* (siphon hoses, buckets, and other utensils) with a specific aquarium (exhibit, quarantine, or treatment). Label dedicated equipment with indelible ink to avoid mix-ups; alternatively, use equipment of different colors, one color for each aquarium. Buckets can be purchased in different colors, and hoses and net handles can be wrapped with matching colored tape.

SIPHONING AN AQUARIUM

Devices to clean aquarium gravel are sold by dealers, although the job can be accomplished easily and efficiently by siphoning. Siphoning is the trickiest part of cleaning an aquarium, but the procedure is easy with a little practice. To practice, fill a dedicated bucket with tap water, set it on the kitchen counter, and siphon water out of the bucket into the sink with the corresponding dedicated siphon hose. Follow Procedure 11. The flow of water through a siphon is controlled by gravity. The dual purposes of siphoning are to remove old water and vacuum out detritus that has accumulated on the surface of the subgravel filter (that is, on top of the gravel). When siphoning the surface of a subgravel filter, the hose must be long enough to reach from the bottom of the aquarium to the bucket (Figure 48).

Procedure 11 *How to Siphon an Aquarium*

1. Remove the aquarium cover.
2. Place one end of the dedicated siphon hose (the source end) in the aquarium and submerge it several inches. Hold it in place with one hand.
3. With your other hand, place a dedicated bucket underneath the receiving end of the hose.
4. Be certain the receiving end is lower than the surface of the water in the aquarium and keep it lower at all times while siphoning.
5. Place the receiving end in your mouth and suck strongly and quickly one time. Use only your mouth to create suction; *do not* inhale through the end as if drawing a deep breath, because you might get water in your lungs.

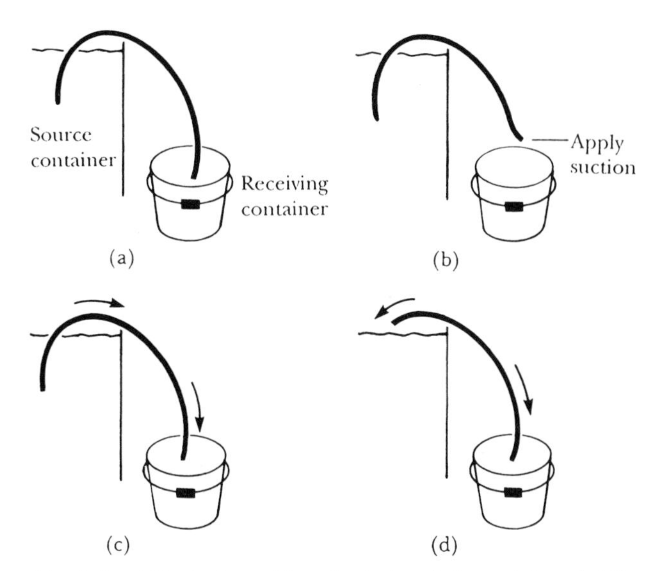

Figure 48 *Sylized illustration of how to start and stop a siphon.* (a) *One end of the siphon hose is placed in the source container (for example, an aquarium) and the other end in a bucket or other receiving container. Notice the difference in elevation between the two ends of hose.* (b) *Apply suction to the receiving end of the hose to start water flowing.* (c) *Allow water to fill the receiving container.* (d) *"Break" or stop the siphon by lifting the source end out of the water and draining the hose into the receiving container.*

6 When water flows freely, submerge the source end to the bottom and start vacuuming detritus. Do not be concerned if a little gravel is also removed; it can be returned to the aquarium later. Continue until the bucket is nearly full.
7 To "break" or interrupt the siphon, remove the source end from the aquarium and allow water remaining in the hose to drain into the bucket.

CLEANING AN AQUARIUM

Procedure 12 outlines the cleaning process. Equipment needed to clean an aquarium is shown in Figure 49 and listed in Table 8. Use only dedicated equipment and beware of mix-ups.

Procedure 12 *How to Clean an Aquarium*

1 Remove the aquarium cover and rinse it in a sink with hot tap water; alternatively, rinse it outdoors with a garden hose. Scrub off biological slime, algae, and salt with the scrub pad and rinse well. Set upright to drain.

Figure 49 *Equipment needed to clean an aquarium: bucket, plastic scrub pad, net for removing debris and detritus, and siphon hose. Not shown are a straightened metal clothes hanger and replacement seawater or artificial seawater.*

TABLE 8 Equipment needed to clean an aquarium; refer to Table 1 for details.

Equipment	Comments
Clean hands and arms	Wash to just above the elbows with ordinary soap, then rinse
Fine-mesh net	Dedicated[1]
Metal clothes hanger	Straightened
Plastic bucket	Dedicated[1]
Plastic scrub pad	Dedicated[1]
Seawater or artificial seawater	Sufficient volume to replace the discarded water
Siphon hose	Dedicated[1]

[1]*Dedicated equipment* is used only with a specific aquarium: the exhibit, quarantine, or treatment aquarium.

2 Unplug the air compressor and immersion heaters. If the immersion heaters are dirty, allow 5 minutes to cool before removing them. *If the immersion heaters are attached to the sides of the aquarium, unplug them even if they are clean. Lowering the water level could expose them to the air, causing the glass cases to crack.*

3 With your hand, scoop the gravel away from the base of each airlift. Uncouple the airline tubing from the rigid plastic tubing inside the airlifts (see Figure 19), then remove the lift tubes from the ports of the subgravel filter (see Figures 18 and 19). Place all pieces in the sink. *Place flower pots upside down over the open ports to keep small animals from entering them.*

4 Carefully remove one decoration with algal growth and place it in the sink. The aquarium habitat is less disrupted if only one piece of décor is removed at each cleaning.

5 Rinse the decoration and immersion heaters with hot tap water and scrub them lightly with the scrub pad to remove algae and biological slime. Rinse again and set aside to drain.

6 Uncouple the head pieces of the airlifts and remove the rigid plastic tubing and air diffusers (see Figures 18 and 19). Rinse these in hot water to loosen algae and biological slime, then scrub them with the scrub pad. Clean the insides of the lift tubes by wadding up a paper towel, wetting it, and shoving it through each tube with a straightened metal clothes hanger. Repeat until the tubes are clean. Afterward, rinse all airlift components and set them aside to drain. Replace clogged air diffusers as necessary (that is, when the flow of water from the airlifts has diminished noticeably).

7 Clean the inside glass surfaces of the aquarium with the scrub pad. Move the gravel aside and clean the glass nearly to the bottom of the aquarium. *Be careful not to pick up gravel grains on the scrub pad because they can scratch the glass.*

8 Detritus tends to collect under the decorations. Turn over a few decorations and gently stir all the aquarium gravel with your hand, but disturb the inhabitants as little as possible. Detritus trapped in the gravel will billow upward. Remove some of the suspended detritus by swishing a fine-mesh net back and forth in a figure-eight pattern. When the net becomes clogged, turn it inside out in the sink and rinse away the detritus with hot tap water. Repeat several times.

9 Stir the gravel again and wait 5 minutes for the remaining detritus to settle. Set up the siphoning apparatus (see Procedure 11). Siphon out as much detritus as possible in combination with the old water.

10 Empty the bucket and repeat until at least 25% of the total volume of water in the aquarium has been removed. The upper 25% level should have been determined in advance and marked permanently with indelible ink on an outside back corner of the aquarium glass (see Chapter 3).

11 Assemble the airlifts and insert them in the ports of the filter plate. Attach the airline tubing and level the gravel so that its depth is the same everywhere. *The fluid flow of water through a subgravel filter follows a path of least resistance, being strongest where the filter plate is exposed. Subgravel filters with exposed sections of filter plate or uneven gravel depth perform inefficiently.*

12 Position the aquarium decorations *exactly* as they were. Shifting their locations—and even their angles of orientation—upsets the social structure of a community aquarium by displacing the inhabitants from familiar shelter spaces.

13 Replace water discarded from the aquarium with an equal volume of new seawater or artificial seawater. Temperatures of replacement and discarded water should be similar ($\pm 5°$ F). Sometimes the new water is much colder. If so, raise the water temperature in the holding container the day before by inserting an immersion heater and supplying mild aeration.

14 Attach the immersion heaters to the inside glass and submerge them to the proper depth (see Figure 37).

15 Set the aquarium cover in place.

16 Plug in the air compressor and immersion heaters.

17 Clean the outside glass all around with a commercial window cleaner *that does not contain ammonia*. Ammonia is toxic to aquarium animals. It is also soluble, and ammonia in the aerosol can enter the aquarium water.

18 Offer your fishes a few live adult brine shrimp (see Chapter 11) to help restore the routine.

ADJUSTING ALKALINITY AND pH

The pH is kept in adjustment partly by continuous, vigorous aeration, which drives off excess carbon dioxide. *However, addition or subtraction of carbon dioxide has no effect on the alkalinity. Consequently, neither does aeration. Without vigorous aeration, a situation can develop in which alkalinity is within the acceptable range of 2.5 to 3.0 mEq/L but the pH declines to below 8.0.* The reaction of carbon dioxide with water produces carbonic acid, which reduces the pH by making the water more acidic (see Figure 28).

Keeping the airlifts performing properly is an important aspect of pH control. As mentioned in Procedure 12, the air diffuser inside an airlift should be replaced when the flow of water emerging from the head piece diminishes noticeably. The aquarist's objective, however, is to keep airlifts operating at maximum capacity around the clock. At maximum capacity, filtered water emerges from the head piece in a strong, smooth stream. Spurting water indicates reduced capacity. Spurting sometimes results from too strong a flow of air. More often, the cause is failure to refill the aquarium to the correct level and keep it there. A low water level impairs airlift performance by causing spurting.

Regular partial water changes assist in pH maintenance by replenishing alkalinity in the form of bicarbonate. Ordinarily, pH adjustments will be upward; excessively high pH values are unusual in conventional marine aquariums. According to one authority,[14] *the pH of seawater or artificial seawater in marine aquariums declines by 0.1 unit or less each week*. Based on this guideline, a pH of 8.2 (the recommended starting pH) will decline to below 8.0 within 3 weeks, at which time an adjustment is necessary. Adjustments are made easily by adding sodium bicarbonate in the form of common baking soda. This practice also replenishes alkalinity. Store opened boxes of baking soda in tightly sealed plastic bags.

[14]See Bower (1980) in Additional Reading ("Beginning and Intermediate Aquarists" section).

Procedure 13 *How to Adjust Alkalinity and pH*

1 Select a pH test kit designed for use with marine aquariums. *Test kits designed to determine* pH in freshwater will give false readings. At the same time, prepare the alkalinity test kit for use.
2 Collect a water sample from the aquarium and determine the alkalinity and pH. *Do not make adjustments unless alkalinity is less than 2.5 mEq/L and the pH is below 8.0.*
3 If alkalinity is within the acceptable range, but the pH is not, increase the rate of aeration. Do nothing else.
4 If both values are too low, follow steps 5 through 9.
5 Submerge a drinking glass (a conventional tumbler) in the aquarium and fill it most of the way.
6 Add approximately 1 teaspoon of baking soda to the tumbler and stir to dissolve.
7 Pour the baking soda solution slowly into the aquarium. The white cloud will disappear instantly.
8 Wait 1 hour and then determine alkalinity and pH.
9 Repeat baking soda additions hourly until the alkalinity is 2.5 to 3.0 mEq/L. If aeration is sufficiently vigorous, the pH should be 8.0 to 8.3. Accidental addition of too much baking soda will not harm the aquarium inhabitants.

ADJUSTING SPECIFIC GRAVITY

Specific gravity can vary with time, either increasing or decreasing. Increases are more common, and the reason ordinarily is evaporation. When water evaporates from a marine aquarium, the concentrations of the remaining constituents increase. This greater "saltiness" is manifested as a higher specific gravity value. Regular partial water changes help maintain stable values between 1.023 and 1.025 at 80°F. A tight-fitting cover also helps by reducing the rate of evaporation.

If specific gravity is low, Open the lid of the aquarium cover and allow evaporation to take place until the next partial water change; if high, adjust the value downward with small amounts of dechlorinated tap water (see Chapter 3). Allow the aquarium to mix thoroughly for 1 hour between additions before making determinations.

CHAPTER

11 Foods and Feeding

Synopsis *Animals that are feeding generalists fare best on the limited dietary items aquarists can offer; feeding specialists should be avoided. Marine animals require dietary proteins, lipids, and tiny amounts of vitamins. Carbohydrates are not necessary in aquarium diets. Minerals, which are important dietary additives for freshwater fishes, are plentiful in seawater and artificial seawaters. No apparent nutritional benefit is gained from feeding plant matter to your aquarium animals. Flake and freeze-dried foods, although readily available, offer no apparent advantage either. Live foods are superior supplements to aquarium diets and extend survival. Adult brine shrimp are the most convenient live foods. They can be purchased from dealers in small quantities. Buy them fresh. At home, rinse brine shrimp in a net to remove bacteria before transferring them to a live food container with aeration. Brine shrimp can be hatched at home from resting cysts (incorrectly called brine shrimp eggs) purchased from dealers. Feed the nauplii to small fishes and invertebrates. Alternatively, rear them to adult size in suitable vessels (for example, plastic garbage cans) using rice bran as food. Adult size is attained in approximately 2 weeks, and cultures can be perpetual; in other words, the brine shrimp will reproduce. Lean fish and other seafoods should also be fed to aquarium animals. Never use leftovers from seafood dinners as aquarium food. Cook all seafoods first by boiling to kill disease organisms. Store frozen and discard when quality declines. Gelatin-based recipes provide superior, inexpensive foods made easily at home. Feed marine aquarium animals small amounts of food at least twice and preferably four times daily. Be sure all specimens get enough to eat and look for signs of weight loss. One way of encouraging all animals in the aquarium to eat properly is to avoid repetitive feeding practices.*

Marine animals eat an astonishing variety of items: algae, detritus, plankton of all sorts, and each other. Some species are more flexible than others in the kinds of foods they select. *Feeding specialists* have little or no choice in their selection of dietary items. For example, certain butterflyfishes and angelfishes eat only coral mucus or live sponges. Evolution dictates what can and will be eaten. When confined in aquariums, feeding specialists ordinarily starve to death despite the presence of other foods. *Feeding generalists* eat a variety of foods in nature. In captivity, this innate flexibility allows them latitude to accept and digest the limited items aquarists can offer. Ease of care—one of five criteria recommended for selecting animals—includes choosing only feeding generalists for community aquariums (see Chapter 8).

FOOD COMPOSITION AND QUALITY

Feeding generalists still require foods containing the necessary nutrients for tissue maintenance, growth, and good health. Marine animals need adequate dietary proteins, lipids (including long-chain polyunsaturated fatty acids), and tiny amounts of vitamins. The few species of fishes tested to date either do not require carbohydrates or can stay healthy on very little. Carbohydrates can be eliminated from aquarium diets. Minerals (actually, inorganic ions), which are important additives in the diets of freshwater fishes, are plentiful in seawater and artificial seawaters.

A varied diet promotes good health in human nutrition, and the diets of captive fishes and invertebrates should be varied for the same reason. Successful aquarists offer a variety of high-quality foods. No apparent nutritional benefit is gained from offering plant matter, even though many fishes and invertebrates are primarily *herbivores* (plant eaters) in nature. Most herbivores, with the possible exception of parrotfishes, adapt quickly to diets composed exclusively of animal matter and become functional *carnivores* (flesh eaters). Plant matter in any form can therefore be eliminated from consideration. Flake and freeze-dried foods, although readily available, offer no apparent advantage either. Many of these products float or break apart quickly when immersed in water. Both characteristics are undesirable.

Live foods are superior to all other nutrient sources for meeting the nutritional requirements of aquarium animals and extending survival. Prepared foods and other sources of nutrients, such as cut fish and shrimp, often have less nutrient value than live brine shrimp. Your success as a marine aquarist—especially with fishes—will be enhanced measurably by including live brine shrimp as a dietary component. And no food matches live brine shrimp for inducing newly acquired fishes to feed.

PURCHASING LIVE ADULT BRINE SHRIMP

The most convenient source of live adult brine shrimp (Figure 50) is the dealer, who sells them by the portion. The size of a *portion* differs according to a dealer's definition, but ordinarily it is a teaspoon of concentrated brine shrimp scooped from a net after the water has been drained away. The contents of the spoon are then transferred to a plastic bag of water for transport home.

Brine shrimp purchased from a dealer vary in quality depending on how long they have been held. From a dealer's perspective, attempting to extend the survival of adult brine shrimp by feeding them is laborious and inconvenient; consequently, nutrient quality diminishes rapidly. *Find out which days of the week your dealer receives shipments of brine shrimp and buy them fresh.*

At home, pour the brine shrimp into a coarse-mesh net and rinse them gently with tap water adjusted to room temperature or slightly cooler. Rinsing removes numerous bacteria, perhaps extending the lives of the brine shrimp and lessening the possibility that infectious disease organisms will be transferred to the aquarium.

Figure 50 *Adult brine shrimp (magnified).* Source: Courtesy Artemia Reference Center, Gent, Belgium.

After rinsing, empty the contents of the net into a live food container of new seawater or artificial seawater. This can be done easily by following Procedure 14. Almost any vessel makes a suitable live food container, but the minimum size should be 1 quart. Plastic mayonnaise jars and similar containers are acceptable. *Adult brine shrimp live longer when not crowded. Use two or more live food containers and limit stocking to 3 teaspoons of concentrated brine shrimp (in other words, three portions) per quart of water.*

Procedure 14 ***How to Transfer Live Adult Brine Shrimp***

1 Fill the live food container almost to the top with new seawater or artificial seawater and set it on the sink near the tap.

2 Empty the plastic bag of brine shrimp obtained from the dealer into a coarse-mesh net. Open the tap to a gentle flow and adjust the temperature to that of the room or slightly cooler. Hold the net under the tap and gently rinse any brine shrimp stuck in the webbing to the bottom of the net (Figure 51). Continue to rinse the brine shrimp for several seconds.

Figure 51 *Empty adult brine shrimp obtained from a dealer into a coarse-mesh net and rinse them in gently flowing tap water of room temperature or slightly cooler.*

PLATE 1

(a) *Juvenile French angelfish* (Pomacanthus paru) *such as this one can be conditioned to accept standard aquarium foods (see Chapter 11). Consequently, captive juveniles often survive and grow. Adults are feeding specialists, subsisting almost entirely on live sponges, and their extended survivorship in captivity is poor (see Chapter 8).*
Bonaire, Netherlands Antilles, 16 feet.

(b) *Compared with adults, juvenile queen angelfish* (Holacanthus ciliaris) *have superior extended survivorship in captivity, in part because they can be conditioned to accept standard aquarium foods (see Chapter 11). Adults are feeding specialists, subsisting almost entirely on live sponges. In captivity, their extended survivorship is poor (see Chapter 8).*
Key Largo, Florida, 18 feet.

(c) *Pygmy angelfishes are readily available to marine aquarists. Many species demonstrate reasonably good extended survivorship in captivity (see Chapter 8). The fish shown are* Centropyge bicolor.
Pertamina Reef, Maumere, Flores, Indonesia, 35 feet.
Source: John E. Randall.

(d) *Juvenile rock beauties* (Holacanthus tricolor) *such as this one often survive and grow in captivity because they can be conditioned to accept standard aquarium foods (see Chapter 11). Adults are feeding specialists, subsisting almost entirely on live sponges, and their extended survivorship in captivity is poor (see Chapter 8).*
Key Largo, Florida, 45 feet.

PLATE 2

(a) *The fairy basslet* (Gramma loreto) *survives well in captivity if brine shrimp nauplii are provided regularly (see Chapter 11) and adequate shelter spaces are available (see Chapter 9). The darkened recess in the background was this fish's shelter space.*
Bonaire, Netherlands Antilles, 95 feet.

(b) *Blennies are interesting and easy to maintain. They require a substratum with lots of small shelter spaces. Species such as this tiny arrow blenny* (Lucayablennius zingaro) *are predators and sometimes require live brine shrimp (see Chapter 11).*
Pine Cay, Turks and Caicos Islands, British West Indies, 45 feet.

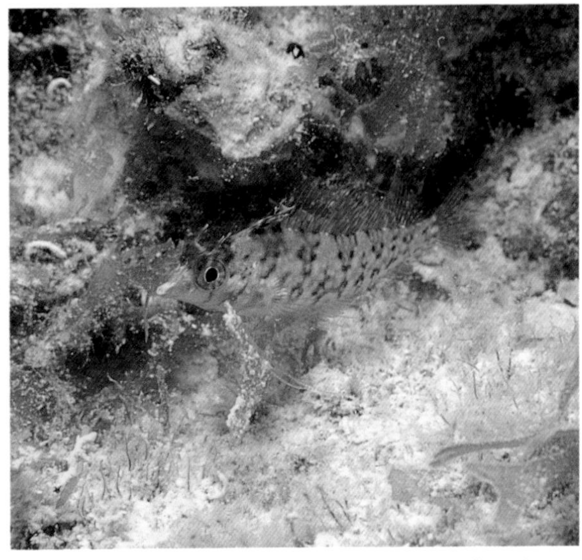

(c) *The saddled blenny* (Malacoctenus triangulatus) *prefers to live on a coral rubble substratum (see Chapter 5). In captivity, brine shrimp nauplii are its preferred food (see Chapter 11).*
Guana Island, British Virgin Islands, 15 feet.

(d) *Other blennies feed on plant material in nature, but most can be conditioned to accept aquarium foods (see Chapter 11). This specimen of* Ecsenius bicolor *was photographed in an area of dense algal growth, and the species might be herbivorous.*
Sabang, Palawan, South China Sea, Philippines, 18 feet.

(a) *Some West Indies butterflyfishes (for example, the foureye butterflyfish,* Chaetodon capistratus) *form temporary pairs at dawn and travel together throughout the day. Adult foureye butterflyfish have poor extended survivorship, as do most butterflyfishes (see Chapter 8), although juveniles can sometimes be maintained if brine shrimp are provided regularly (see Chapter 11).*
Key Largo, Florida, 30 feet.

(b) Chaetodon baronessa *is sometimes seen in pairs but commonly travels alone. Like most butterflyfishes, this species has poor extended survivorship in captivity (see Chapter 8).*
Coco Loco Island, Palawan, Sulu Sea, Philippines, 22 feet (night).

(c) *The barberfish* (Heniochus nigrirostris) *is a butterflyfish that lives in large groups and feeds on plankton (see Chapter 13).*
Cabo San Lucas, Baja California, Mexico, 55 feet.

(d) Heniochus chrysostomus *is often solitary or found in pairs. Specimens seldom appear in the marine aquarium trade.*
Sabang, Palawan, South China Sea, Philippines, 50 feet.

(a) *Cardinalfishes are nocturnal. This fish is a pale cardinalfish* (Apogon planifrons). *In aquariums, cardinalfishes often hide in shelter spaces during the day (see Chapter 13). Many species can be conditioned to feed in daylight hours but sometimes fare better if brine shrimp nauplii are provided just before the lights are turned out.*
Pine Cay, Turks and Caicos Islands, British West Indies, 33 feet (night).

(b) *Most damselfishes are small, active, and accept a variety of foods. Anemonefishes ordinarily are peaceful. If a sea anemone is present, it is used as a permanent shelter space. This fish is a female* Amphiprion frenatus; *the sea anemone is* Entacmaea quadricolor.
Tres Marias, Ulugan Bay, Palawan, South China Sea, Philippines, 54 feet.

(c) *Many species of damselfishes defend territories on coral reefs (see Chapter 13). Among the most belligerent is the beaugregory* (Pomacentrus leucostictus). *The specimens shown are juveniles.*
Caicos Bank, Turks and Caicos Islands, British West Indies, 5 feet.

(d) *Adult threespot damselfish* (Pomacentrus planifrons) *survive well in aquariums but are territorial and aggressive (see Chapter 13). If you decide to maintain adults of this species, keep only one specimen. The seaweed is* Caulerpa racemosa, *an ornamental alga (see Chapter 14).*
Grand Anse Bay, Grenada, West Indies, 47 feet.

PLATE 5

(a) *Some adult bicolor damselfish* (Pomacentrus partitus) *are territorial; others live peacefully in large colonies (see Chapter 13). This adult is solitary and defending a territory.*
Bonaire, Netherlands Antilles, 37 feet.

(b) *The longfin damselfish* (Pomacentrus diencaeus) *defends its territory aggressively (see Chapter 13). This specimen is an adult.*
Key Largo, Florida, 33 feet.

(c) *Dottybacks resemble damselfishes. Several species are commonly available in the marine aquarium trade. The fish shown is* Pseudochromis diadema.
Batangas, Luzon, Philippines, 70 feet.
Source: John E. Randall.

(d) Dactylopus dactylopus *belongs to the dragonettes, a group of small, bottom-dwelling fishes.*
Maumere Bay, Flores, Indonesia, 45 feet.
Source: John E. Randall.

PLATE 6

(a) *The spotted drum* (Equetus punctatus) *is peaceful, shy, accepts most foods offered, and needs adequate shelter space (see Chapter 13). This specimen is an adult, but juveniles are usually available in the marine aquarium trade. The sea anemone is* Condylactis gigantea.
Rocher du Diamont, Martinique, French West Indies, 90 feet.

(b) *The sea catfish* (Plotsus lineatus), *one of the eeltail catfishes, is a schooling species with mildly venomous spines. Its extended survivorship is good (see Chapter 8), and it accepts most aquarium foods (see Chapter 11).*
Coco Loco Island, Sulu Sea, Philippines, 18 feet.

(c) *Filefishes ordinarily are poor choices for small community aquariums (see Chapter 13). Many species attain large size quickly and feed aggressively on invertebrates, especially crustaceans and sea urchins. The fish shown is a whitespotted filefish* (Cantherhines macroceros).
Pine Cay, Turks and Caicos Islands, British West Indies, 48 feet.

(d) *Gobies are mostly small, unobtrusive aquarium inhabitants. Many will accept seafoods and gelatin-based foods (see Chapter 11) but often prefer brine shrimp nauplii. These neon gobies* (Gobiosoma oceanops) *are occupying a brain coral* (Colpophyllia natans).
Key Largo, Florida, 32 feet.

PLATE 7

(a) *In captivity, the bridled goby* (Coryphopterus glaucofraenum) *prefers a coral rubble substratum (see Chapter 5) containing numerous small shelter spaces. Stirring the substratum during routine maintenance (see Chapter 10) disrupts the daily activities of gobies and other small aquarium animals by destroying their shelter spaces.*
Guana Island, British Virgin Islands, 8 feet.

(b) *Sea basses ordinarily are poor choices for community aquariums. Many species quickly outgrow most home aquariums, although not without first consuming some of the smaller inhabitants. Hamlets are exceptions. Ichthyologists (fish specialists) consider the different color variants to be a single species,* Hypoplectrus unicolor. *The fish shown is a yellowbelly hamlet.*
Key Largo, Florida, 27 feet.

(c) *The tiny chalk bass* (Serranus tortugarum) *is peaceful. In captivity, it prefers to live on a coral rubble substratum (see Chapter 5) and readily accepts brine shrimp nauplii.*
Guana Island, British Virgin Islands, 65 feet.

(d) *Anthiines are peaceful and often strikingly colored. This fish is an adult male* Pseudanthias pleurotaenia. *Adult females of the species are yellow.*
Menjangen, Bali, Indonesia, 100 feet.
Source: John E. Randall.

(a) *The redspotted hawkfish* (Amblycirrhitus pinos) *is peaceful and often "perches" on objects. If startled it darts into a crevice. Many hawkfishes accept seafoods and gelatin-based foods (see Chapter 11), although newly acquired specimens sometimes accept only brine shrimp.*
Bonaire, Netherlands Antilles, 12 feet.

(b) *The yellowhead jawfish* (Opistognathus aurifrons) *digs a burrow in the substratum, which is used as a nocturnal shelter space (see Chapter 9). Yellowhead jawfish feed on plankton during the day (see Chapter 13) but never venture far from their burrows. In captivity, all jawfishes need a substratum at least 3 inches deep of mixed coral hash, coral gravel, and coral rubble (see Chapters 5 and 8).*
Bonaire, Netherlands Antilles, 35 feet.

(c) *Among the most spectacular coral reef fishes is the moorish idol* (Zanclus cornutus), *but its extended survivorship in captivity is poor (see Chapter 8).*
Kwajalein, Marshall Islands, 40 feet.
Source: John E. Randall.

(d) *The predatory habits of some morays make them poor choices for community aquariums (see Chapter 8). All require adequate shelter space (see Chapter 9), which is sometimes difficult to provide for large specimens. The green moray* (Gymnothorax funebris) *in this photograph was at least 5 feet in length.*
Bonaire, Netherlands Antilles, 85 feet.

PLATE 9

(a) *Roundheads have excellent extended survivorship in captivity (see Chapter 8). This fish is* Calloplesiops altivelis.
Gulf of Aqaba, Red Sea, 25 feet.
Source: John E. Randall.

(b) *The barbfish* (Scorpaena brasiliensis) *is a scorpionfish. Scorpionfishes are not good choices for community aquariums. They prey on smaller inhabitants (see Chapter 8), and some of their spines are venomous and potentially dangerous to aquarists.*
Key Largo, Florida, 27 feet.

(c) *The turkeyfish* (Pterois volitans) *is a scorpionfish, and some of its spines are venomous. Turkeyfishes can be conditioned to accept seafoods and gelatin-based foods (see Chapter 11), although live foods (preferably live fishes) should be offered once weekly.*
Tres Marias, Ulugan Bay, Palawan, South China Sea, Philippines, 45 feet.

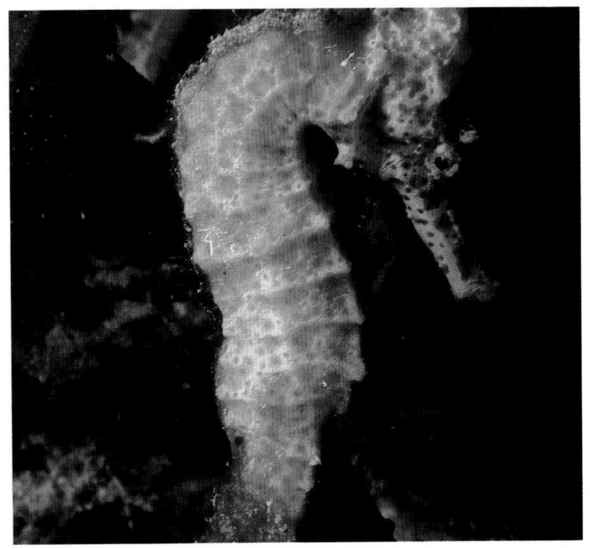

(d) *The lined seahorse* (Hippocampus erectus) *is a peaceful, interesting inhabitant of community aquariums. However, it steadfastly refuses to accept nonliving foods and requires live adult brine shrimp (see Chapter 11). Without live foods, starvation is inevitable.*
Bonaire, Netherlands Antilles, 57 feet.

(a) *The squirrelfish* (Holocentrus rufus) *is shy and nocturnal but often emerges from its shelter space during the day, as this specimen has done. Squirrelfishes accept seafoods and gelatin-based foods (see Chapter 11). Large specimens sometimes prey on other aquarium inhabitants (see Chapter 8). Key Largo, Florida, 37 feet.*

(b) *The glasseye snapper* (Priacanthus cruentatus) *is shy, nocturnal, and needs adequate shelter space. It accepts seafoods and gelatin-based foods (see Chapter 11) and sometimes preys on smaller inhabitants of community aquariums. Key Largo, Florida, 28 feet.*

(c) *The blue tang* (Acanthurus coeruleus) *is yellow as a juvenile. Surgeonfishes and tangs are peaceful in community aquariums and demonstrate good extended survivorship. They ordinarily accept all foods. Bonaire, Netherlands Antilles, 58 feet.*

(d) *Many surgeonfishes and tangs school as adults (see Chapter 13). These are yellowtail surgeonfish* (Prionurus punctatus).
Cabo San Lucas, Baja California, Mexico, 67 feet.

(a) *Small wrasses adapt well to community aquariums. Many species burrow into the substratum at night, and aquariums containing wrasses should have a substratum consisting of coral hash at least 3 inches deep (see Chapters 5 and 8). Juvenile specimens of* Coris gaimard *appear commonly in the marine aquarium trade.*
Negros, Philippines, 30 feet.
Source: John E. Randall.

(b) *This wrasse is an adult Spanish hogfish* (Bodianus rufus). *Juveniles are similar in appearance. Wrasses ordinarily have excellent extended survivorship in captivity (see Chapter 8) and accept most foods.*
Bonaire, Netherlands Antilles, 42 feet.

(c) *The creole wrasse* (Clepticus parrae) *is social, feeding in groups on plankton in the water column above coral reefs (see Chapter 13). In captivity, most planktivorous fishes prefer live brine shrimp (see Chapter 11).*
Bonaire, Netherlands Antilles, 95 feet.

(d) *Anemone shrimps live in association with sea anemones. This shrimp is* Periclimenes yucatanicus; *the sea anemone is* Condylactis gigantea. *Anemone shrimps can survive in captivity indefinitely without a sea anemone but are more likely to be eaten by predatory fishes.*
Bonaire, Netherlands Antilles, 18 feet.

PLATE 12

(a) *The red coral shrimp* (Rhynchocinetes ringens) *is nocturnal. It survives well in aquariums but is seldom seen if adequate shelter space is available.*
Bonaire, Netherlands Antilles, 55 feet (night).

(b) *The arrow crab* (Stenorhynchus seticornis) *is nocturnal. Like most crabs, it accepts a variety of foods and has good extended survivorship in captivity (see Chapter 8).*
Bonaire, Netherlands Antilles, 30 feet (night).

(c) *Hermit crabs accept most aquarium foods and demonstrate excellent extended survivorship in captivity (see Chapter 8). The crab shown* (Paguristes punticeps) *is nocturnal.*
Anguilla Cay, Bahamas, 35 feet (night).

(d) *The claws of the shame-faced crab* (Calappa flammea) *cover its face. The species is nocturnal, emerging after dusk to feed on detritus, algae, and small invertebrates. Most crabs accept a variety of aquarium foods and demonstrate excellent extended survivorship in captivity (see Chapter 8).*
Pine Cay, Turks and Caicos Islands, British West Indies, 8 feet (night).

PLATE 13

(a) *Sea anemones that require bright light are difficult to maintain in conventional marine aquariums (see Chapter 14). They shrink over a period of weeks under inadequate illumination and eventually die. Life on coral reefs is intensely competitive. This sea anemone* (Condylactis gigantea) *has stung and killed the live coral within reach of its tentacles.*
Bonaire, Netherlands Antilles, 52 feet.

(b) *The corallimorpharians, or coral-like anemones, also seem to require supplemental light (see Chapter 14) for survival, even though they often inhabit deep reefs where the light is dim. This colony of* Rhodactis sanctithomae *sheltered a small commensal crab.*
Rocher du Diamont, Martinique, French West Indies, 100 feet.

(c) Pseudocorynactis caribbeorum *is a nocturnal corallimorpharian. During the day it stays hidden in a crevice in the reef.*
Bonaire, Netherlands Antilles, 90 feet (night).

(d) *Live corals are not good candidates for conventional marine aquariums because of poor extended survivorship (see Chapter 8). The orange tube coral* (Tubastrea aurea) *is sometimes an exception. The polyps expand at night, and colonies can occasionally be maintained on brine shrimp nauplii added just before the lights are turned out.*
Bonaire, Netherlands Antilles, 30 feet (night).

(a) *Some sea stars feed on attached algae, although most species available to aquarists are carnivores and accept seafoods and gelatin-based foods (see Chapter 11).* Astropecten duplicatus *is nocturnal, emerging from beneath the sediment at night.*
Pine Cay, Turks and Caicos Islands, British West Indies, 9 feet (night).

(b) *The sea urchin* Lytechinus variegatus *often covers its upper surface with pieces of vegetation or coral rubble. This unusual behavior has not been explained.*
Bonaire, Netherlands Antilles, 17 feet.

(c) *Most mollusks are difficult to maintain in conventional marine aquariums. The rough lima* (Lima scabra) *probably feeds on plankton and suspended detritus. Consequently, its extended survivorship in captivity is poor (see Chapter 8).*
Bonaire, Netherlands Antilles, 85 feet (night).

(d) *Many nudibranchs (also called sea slugs) are feeding specialists (see Chapters 8 and 11); for example, some species consume only live sea anemones or hydroids. Consequently, their extended survivorship in captivity is poor.* Tidachia crispata *feeds on algae and occasionally survives in aquariums with supplemental light (see Chapter 14).*
Florida Bay, Key Largo, Florida, 4 feet.

(a) *The Spanish shawl* (Flabellinopsis iodinea) *is a feeding specialist with poor extended survivorship in captivity (see Chapters 8 and 11). Dealers sometimes place Spanish shawls and other cool-water nudibranchs in tropical aquariums, which further reduces their prospects of survival. The colonial sea anemones are* Corynactis californicus.
Paradise Cove, Malibu, California, 24 feet.

(b) *Annelids (segmented worms) are not discussed in the text, although dealers sometimes stock them. The fire worm* (Hermodice carunculata) *scavenges, but it also preys on sea anemones, corals, and other invertebrates. The specimen shown was consuming a live sea whip. The white bristles are filled with venom.*
Pine Cay, Turks and Caicos Islands, British West Indies, 32 feet (night).

(c) *The Venus cup* (Acetabularia calyculus) *is an attractive ornamental alga (see Chapter 14). It survives and grows well in aquariums if supplemental light is provided.*
Florida Bay, Key Largo, Florida, 3 feet.

(d) Caulerpa verticillata, *an ornamental alga (see Chapter 14), requires supplemental light when kept in aquariums, although it occurs in nature to depths of nearly 100 feet, where the light is dim.*
Pine Cay, Turks and Caicos Islands, British West Indies, 47 feet.

PLATE 16

(a) Caulerpa sertularioides *is an attractive ornamental alga (see Chapter 14) that survives well under supplemental light.*
Caicos Bank, Turks and Caicos Islands, British West Indies, 5 feet.

(b) *The ornamental alga* Stypopodium zonale *(see Chapter 14) is one of the brown algae. It requires supplemental light when kept in aquariums, although the species occurs in nature to depths of at least 240 feet, where the light is very dim.*
Pine Cay, Turks and Caicos Islands, British West Indies, 37 feet.

(c) *Contrary to popular opinion, marine aquariums overgrown with spontaneous algae (see Chapter 14) are not reminiscent of coral reefs. They more closely resemble shallow bays and mangrove habitats, such as the scene in this photograph.*
Florida Bay, Key Marathon, Florida, 5 feet.

(d) *Coral reefs vary enormously in appearance, although they never resemble the scene depicted in Plate 16c. For example, spectacular crinoids (relatives of sea stars and sea urchins) are typical inhabitants of some Indo-West Pacific coral reefs. In captivity, crinoids demonstrate poor extended survivorship.*
Tres Marias, Ulugan Bay, Philippines, South China Sea, 50 feet.

3 Hold the bottom of the net (the section containing the brine shrimp) in one hand and turn the net upside down over the live food container.
4 Immerse the bottom of the net completely in the water of the container and allow the brine shrimp to drift free (Figure 52). Poke the net down with your fingers until the whole lower section is submerged.
5 Move the net gently up and down two or three times to dislodge any brine shrimp stuck to the webbing.
6 Place the live food container on a flat surface and insert a length of airline tubing with a weighted air diffuser (see Figure 12).
7 Adjust the air flow to provide gentle aeration. This is best accomplished by use of gang valves (see Figure 4). Such an arrangement allows two or more containers to be aerated simultaneously (Figure 53). The brine shrimp should drift slowly in the current established by aeration. Violent aeration serves no useful purpose.

Figure 52 *Transfer adult brine shrimp to the live food container by turning the net upside down, immersing it in the water, and allowing the brine shrimp to drift free. Move the net up and down several times to dislodge any brine shrimp stuck to the webbing.*

Figure 53 *Two live food containers can be aerated simultaneously with a single air compressor. These containers each hold 1 quart. Product endorsement is not implied.*

8 Do not keep adult brine shrimp longer than 5 days.
9 Wash empty live food containers with hot tap water and mild soap (not detergent). Rinse well and set aside to drain.

HATCHING BRINE SHRIMP RESTING CYSTS

Brine shrimp can be hatched from *resting cysts* (also called *cysts*) and used either as food or reared to adult size at home. "Brine shrimp eggs" is not an appropriate term because resting cysts are not eggs but embryos in arrested development. Larval brine shrimp (Figure 54), or *nauplii* (the singular is *nauplius*), ordinarily are too small for feeding to large fishes and invertebrates. However, they are excellent food for sea anemones, shrimps, and small fishes such as juvenile butterflyfishes and angelfishes and adult gobies and blennies. Species that feed heavily on *zooplankton* (animal plankton) in nature are *planktivores*. They too fare well on brine shrimp nauplii. Many juvenile and adult damselfishes (including anemonefishes, or clownfishes) are planktivores.

Brine shrimp cysts hatched at home provide food for immediate use and serve as a potential source of adult brine shrimp for larger aquarium animals. Brine shrimp cysts can be purchased

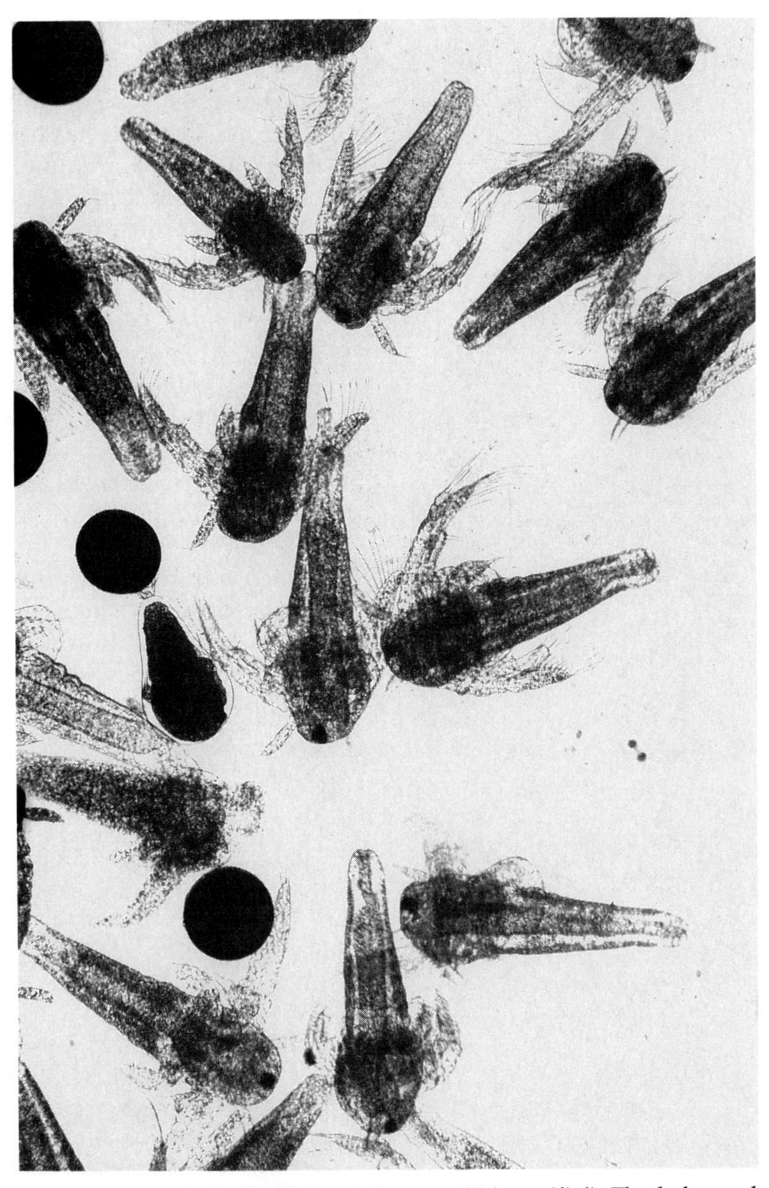

Figure 54 *Newly hatched brine shrimp nauplii (magnified). The dark round objects are unhatched cysts.* Sources: Osborn Laboratories of Marine Sciences and New York Zoological Society, reprinted with permission; also S. Spotte, *Marine Aquarium Keeping: The Science, Animals, and Art,* John Wiley & Sons, Inc., © 1973, reprinted with permission.

from dealers. The container will have been vacuum sealed (Figure 55), and cysts that have been packaged properly can survive in an arrested state of embryonic development for many years. After the container has been opened, the cysts absorb moisture from the air. A warm, moist environment promotes the growth of bacteria and fungi. These organisms attack the cysts and kill them. For this reason, previously opened containers should be closed tightly and stored in a refrigerator between uses. *Cyst survival in containers that have been opened is extended by refrigeration.*

Embryonic development resumes when resting cysts are *wetted* (placed in water) in the presence of light. Continuous light is unnecessary, provided the hatch vessel is illuminated strongly for 10 minutes starting shortly after the cysts have been wetted. Most cysts will hatch within 24 hours at 80°F, and hatching time can be shortened by raising the temperature even higher. Newly hatched nauplii survive for the first 24 hours or so on yolk retained from the cyst. The yolk is high in nutrients, and unabsorbed yolk adds measurably to the nutrient value of a nauplius. Not surprisingly, the nutrient quality of nauplii declines as the yolk is absorbed. If brine shrimp nauplii are to be fed to aquarium animals, they should be separated and used soon after hatching; nauplii older than 24 hours are best reared to adult size, as described in the next section.

Figure 55 *Brine shrimp resting cysts (sometimes wrongly labeled "brine shrimp eggs") can be purchased in sealed containers. Refrigerate the container after opening to prevent the growth of bacteria and fungi. Product endorsement is not implied.* Source: San Francisco Bay Brand Inc., 8239 Enterprise Drive, Newark CA 94560.

Figure 56 *Brine shrimp cysts can be hatched in any convenient container, although a glass gallon jug works well.* Source: S. Spotte, *Marine Aquarium Keeping: The Science, Animals, and Art,* John Wiley & Sons, Inc., © 1973, reprinted with permission.

Brine shrimp cysts can be hatched in containers of all sorts, including gallon jugs (Figure 56). If the design of the hatch vessel is simple, clear glass containers are superior for separating the newly hatched nauplii from the cyst shells and debris. This is because brine shrimp are *photopositive;* that is, they swim toward light. The most common method of concentrating nauplii for later removal is to shine a point source of light at a right angle to the hatch vessel. Opaque containers work less well in this respect because the light is diffused. Equipment and supplies are listed in Table 9.

TABLE 9 Equipment and supplies for hatching brine shrimp cysts.

Air compressor (small)
Air diffuser (weighted)
Airline tubing for aeration
Airline tubing for siphoning
Brine shrimp cysts
Brine shrimp net or sieve (sized for nauplii)
Bucket
Gang valves
Hatch vessel
Immersion heater (25 watt)
Incandescent lamp (100 watt)
Live food container (1 quart)
Plastic measuring spoons (teaspoon only)
Seawater or artificial seawater
Small flashlight with narrow beam

Procedure 15 ***How to Hatch Brine Shrimp Cysts***

1. Purchase a sealed container of brine shrimp cysts from a dealer. *After the seal has been broken, close the container tightly and store in a refrigerator.*
2. Select a *hatch vessel* holding approximately 1 gal (a glass gallon jug is used in this example).
3. Set up the hatch vessel in a warm location; otherwise, insert a small (25-watt) immersion heater and adjust the temperature to 80°F or slightly higher.
4. Add new seawater or artificial seawater. The amount is unimportant, but use most of the volume of the container.
5. Add 1 level teaspoon of brine shrimp cysts.
6. Drop in a weighted air diffuser with a length of airline tubing.
7. Attach the airline tubing to a gang valve (See Figure 4); attach the valve to the air compressor with another length of airline tubing.
8. Adjust the air flow to provide moderately intense aeration.
9. Illuminate the hatch vessel for 10 minutes to stimulate embryonic development. A standard room lamp with a 100-watt incandescent bulb placed 6 inches from the hatch vessel is adequate. *If the hatch vessel is not aerated during this step, some cysts will be shielded from the light.*
10. After 24 to 36 hours, remove the air diffuser and prepare to separate the nauplii. If an immersion heater has been used, unplug it and allow 5 minutes to cool before removing it.

Steps 10 through 16 are shown diagrammatically in Figure 57.

11 Leave the hatch vessel undisturbed for 30 minutes. During this time, most of the cyst debris will rise to the top; the remainder will sink to the bottom.

12 Turn out the room lights and shine a point-source of light (for example, a flashlight with a narrow beam) into the center of the hatch vessel at a right angle. Devise a bracket to

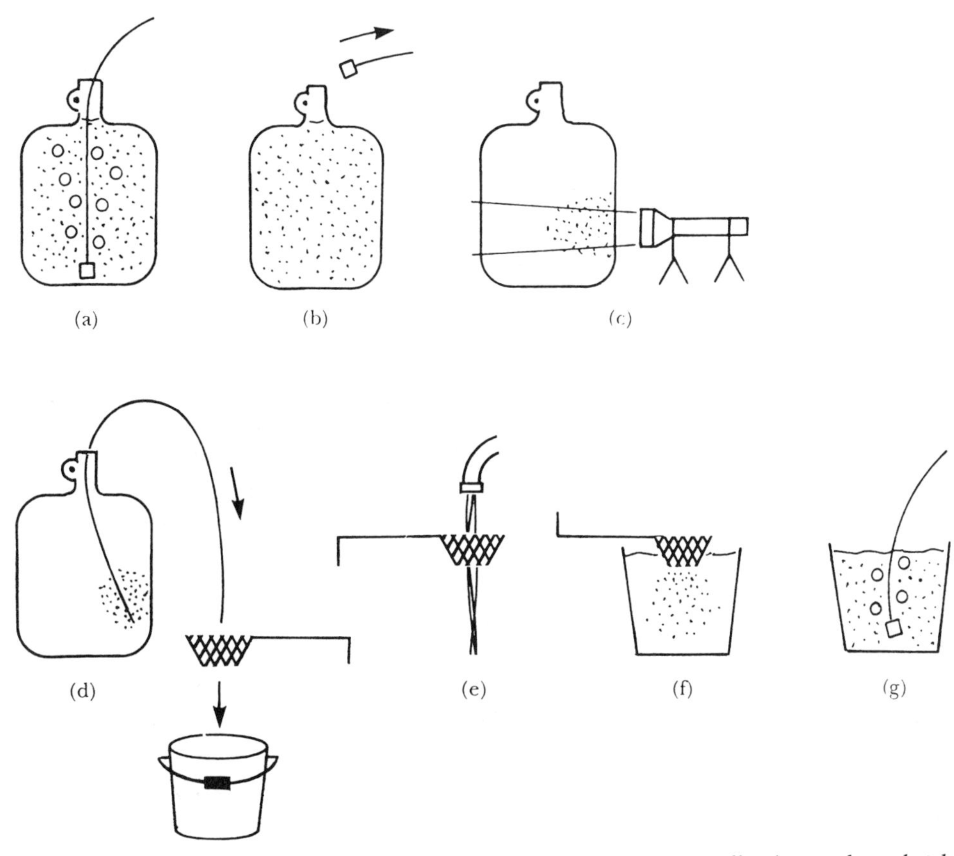

Figure 57 *Removal and transfer of brine shrimp nauplii from a glass gallon jug used as a hatch vessel.* (a) *Nauplii are dispersed while the hatch vessel is being aerated.* (b) *Removing the air diffuser allows nauplii and cyst debris to separate.* (c) *The beam from a flashlight mounted in a bracket is aimed perpendicular to the jug. Brine shrimp are photopositive and will swim toward the light source.* (d) *When the brine shrimp have concentrated in one location, siphon them into a net or sieve through a length of airline tubing. The bucket is to catch the water.* (e) *Wash the nauplii gently in tap water of room temperature or slightly cooler.* (f) *Turn the net upside down over a live food container filled with new seawater or artificial seawater and immerse it to release the nauplii.* (g) *Provide mild aeration until the nauplii are used as food.*

hold the flashlight at a distance of 1 or 2 inches. The nauplii will swim toward the light.

13 After 30 minutes, carefully insert a length of airline tubing into the mass of concentrated nauplii. Try not to disturb the water because cyst debris will begin to disperse and mingle with the nauplii. *The goal is to siphon only the nauplii and leave cyst debris behind.*

14 Siphon the nauplii into a net or sieve made specifically for brine shrimp nauplii. These are sold by dealers. Standard aquarium nets are too coarse to retain newly hatched brine shrimp. Hold the net or sieve over a bucket to catch the water. *Try not to siphon cyst debris.*

15 Rinse the nauplii gently in the net or sieve with tap water adjusted to room temperature or slightly cooler, then transfer them to a live food container (no larger than 1 quart) of clean seawater or artificial seawater. If using a net, turn it inside out, submerge it in the container, and allow the nauplii to drift free. Move the net up and down gently two or three times to release any nauplii stuck to the webbing. If a sieve is used, invert it over the container and flush the nauplii off the screen with a little seawater or artificial seawater.

16 Place a weighted air diffuser (see Figure 12) in the container and aerate gently.

17 If some of the nauplii are to be used as food, take the container to a sink and pour part of the water into another net or sieve made for brine shrimp nauplii. Rinse again with tap water and transfer the nauplii to the aquarium using the technique in step 15. *A net used in this step should be dedicated; that is, each aquarium should have its own. The sieve does not have to be dedicated unless the brine shrimp nauplii are washed off by immersing the sieve in the aquarium.*

18 Empty the hatch vessel and wash it with hot tap water and mild soap (not detergent). Rinse well and drain.

REARING BRINE SHRIMP TO ADULT SIZE

Brine shrimp can be reared to a length of approximately 1/2 inch in 2 weeks. With patience and sufficient space, a brine shrimp culture can be perpetual. A *perpetual culture* is established by leaving enough adults in the rearing vessels to reproduce. The cysts shed into the water hatch and provide nauplii continuously. The benefit is a steady supply of adult brine shrimp of good nutrient quality. Both the rearing vessel design and feeding method described here were devised by Romeo Liwag of Quezon City, Philippines. Mr. Liwag graciously outlined his methods for me when I visited the Philippines in May 1991.

Food quality is important in the rearing of brine shrimp, but less so than food availability. Brine shrimp are able to grow and reproduce normally on low-grade food sources. However, they feed on food particles that are suspended in the water, not lying on the bottom. Brine shrimp *graze* (feed more or less continuously), and the amount of food ingested depends on the number of particles in suspension. The foods offered must be sufficiently small to be ingested and low enough in density to be kept suspended by aeration. Large particles sink to the bottom of the rearing vessel, where they are unavailable. *If food quality is adequate, growth and reproduction of brine shrimp are limited by food availability.*

The enormous amounts of food required by a thriving brine shrimp culture add substantially to the pollutant load. Brine shrimp are extremely tolerant of polluted water, but even they have limits. Poor water quality is the most common cause of failure. The design of rearing vessels obviously requires some thought.

To make the best use of floor space, large numbers of brine shrimp must be reared in relatively small volumes of water. Plastic garbage cans holding 30 gal are useful. Set up at least three and raise them several inches above the floor for convenient siphoning. Sheets of plywood on cinder blocks make suitable platforms. Temperature control is important. If the space is cold, as in a garage, basement, or workshop, supply at least 6 watts of heat per gallon to maintain water temperatures at 83 to 88°F. Large aquarium immersion heaters perform capably. Light is not important, and the tops of the cans may be covered or left exposed.

Biological filtration should be provided to help sustain reasonably good water quality. Its primary function in this situation is the conversion of ammonia. Subgravel filters are impractical because they quickly become clogged with food particles. In addition, brine shrimp become trapped among the gravel grains. Plastic filtrants of any shape and size (for example, rings or cylinders) ordinarily are used because they are porous enough for brine shrimp to circulate through (Figure 58). Contrary to advertisements for these products in the marine aquarium literature, there is no experimental evidence indicating that one plastic filtrant design is demonstrably superior to any other. Simply purchase enough material to fill the bottom third of each rearing

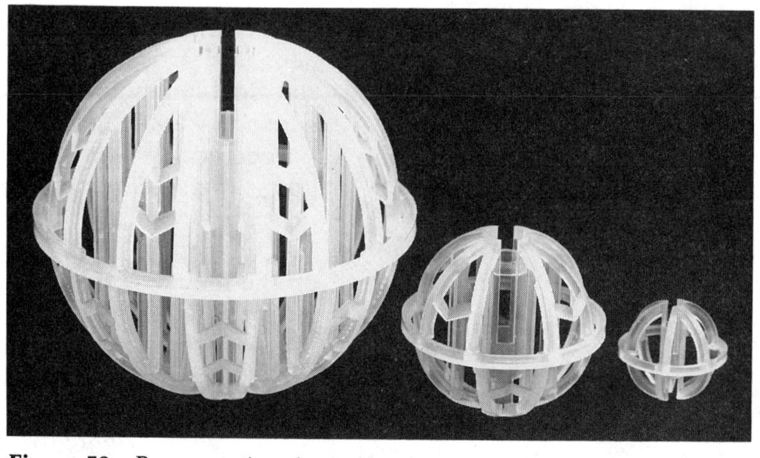

Figure 58 *Representative plastic filtrant. Product endorsement is not implied.* Source: Jaeger Products, Inc., 1611 Peach Leaf, Houston TX 77039.

vessel (Figure 59). I recommend using plastic filtrants having a diameter of 1 inch.

Brine shrimp have been reared on many types of foods, although rice bran is inexpensive, available, easy to use, and effective. Health food stores sell rice bran as brown rice flour and usually display it in the refrigerated section (Figure 60). Buy the finest grind (smallest particle size) and store tightly sealed in a

TABLE 10 Equipment and supplies for rearing brine shrimp to adult size.

Air compressor of large capacity
Airline tubing
Coarse-mesh net
Gang valves
Immersion heaters (6 watts/gal if the room is cold)
Large air diffusers (6)
Plastic filtrant (enough to fill bottom third of each rearing vessel)
Rearing vessels: 30-gal plastic garbage cans (3)
Rice bran
Scissors and string
Seawater or artificial seawater (approximately 75 gal)
Siphon hose
Squares of cloth folded to double thickness

Source: Based on instructions supplied by Romeo Liwag, Quezon City, Philippines.

refrigerator. Even fine-grade rice bran contains numerous large particles. Procedure 16 describes how to keep them out of the rearing vessels. Equipment and supplies for rearing brine shrimp are listed in Table 10.

Procedure 16 *How to Rear Brine Shrimp to Adult Size*

1. Set three 30-gal plastic garbage cans on raised platforms. Allow sufficient working space. These are the *rearing vessels*.
2. Purchase six large air diffusers (Figure 61); three will be spares. These are sold by dealers. Also required are at least one air compressor of large capacity, some airline tubing, and gang valves (see Figure 4). The air diffusers should not need to be weighted. Connect the air diffusers to lengths of airline tubing and place one in each rearing vessel.

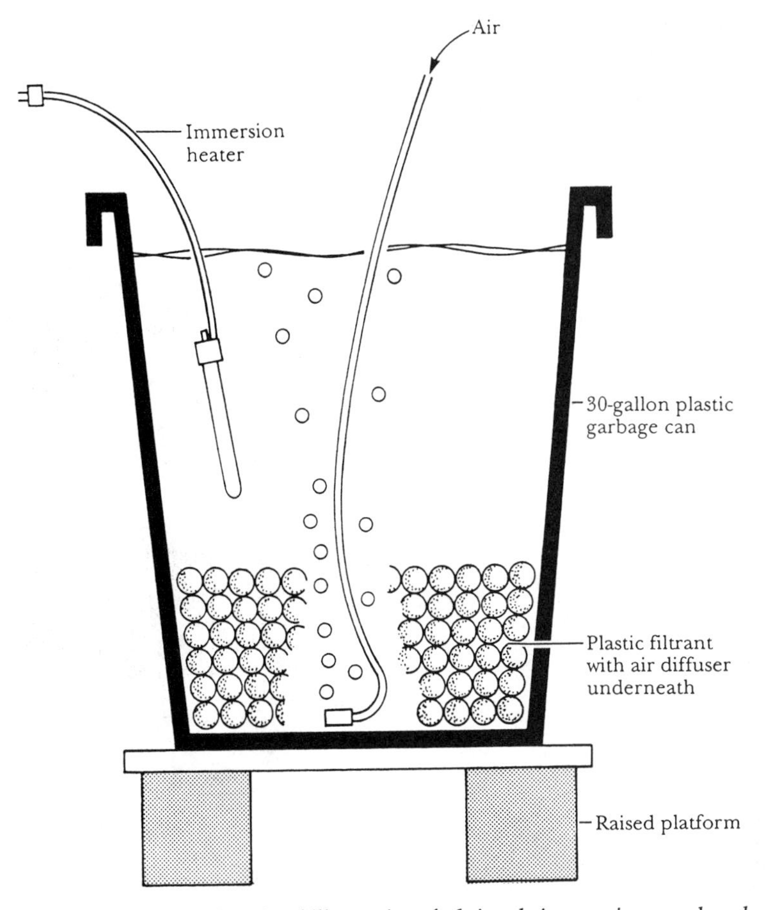

Figure 59 *Stylized sectional illustration of a brine shrimp rearing vessel made from a 30-gal plastic garbage can.*

Figure 60 *Rice bran as brown rice flour is sold at health food stores and usually displayed in the refrigerated section. Product endorsement is not implied.*

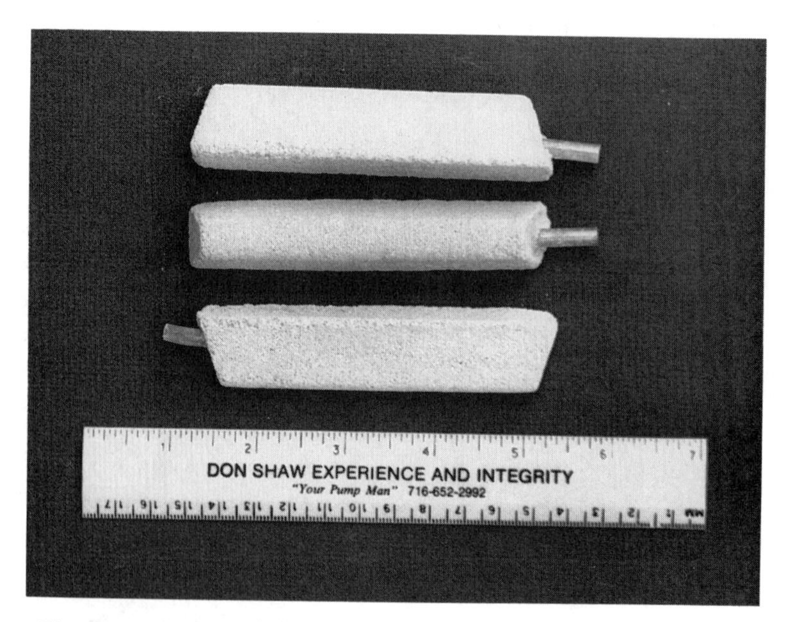

Figure 61 *Large air diffusers used to aerate brine shrimp rearing vessels.*

3. Fill the bottom third of the rearing vessels with plastic filtrant (see Figure 59). The functions of aeration are to (1) enhance gas transfer and (2) keep food particles suspended and available to the brine shrimp. *The air diffusers must therefore be placed at the very bottoms of the rearing vessels (underneath the plastic filtrant). Otherwise, particles that drift to the bottom cannot be resuspended.*
4. Fill the rearing vessels nearly to the top with seawater or artificial seawater.
5. Plug in the air compressor and adjust the air flow to a vigorous rate. Use gang valves to distribute the flow of air evenly.
6. Insert the immersion heaters and adjust the temperature to 83 to 88°F.
7. Add to each rearing vessel all nauplii obtained from 1 level teaspoon of cysts. Afterward, the tops of the rearing vessels may be covered or left exposed.
8. Heap approximately 3 tablespoons of rice bran onto the center of a square of thick cloth (Figure 62). A piece cut from an old shirt works well. To gain thickness, fold the cloth before cutting it. Thickness is important because the cloth must act as a filter by retaining large rice bran particles.
9. Fold the edges of the cloth to form a tight ball with the rice bran at the center. Tie the ends with string (Figure 63).
10. Dip the ball in a rearing vessel to wet it thoroughly, then squeeze once to release a milky cloud of fine rice bran particles. Allow a minute or two for the cloud to disperse. If necessary, squeeze again until the water appears slightly milky. *Do not overfeed. This cannot be emphasized too strongly. Overfeeding is the main reason why brine shrimp cultures fail.*
11. Feed the nauplii in the other rearing vessels, then place the ball of rice bran on a plate and refrigerate. Each ball lasts for several feedings.
12. When the water begins to clear in a day or two, repeat the procedure. *The water clears faster as the brine shrimp grow and consume more food.*
13. Replace 25% of the water weekly. To remove old water, siphon from the *bottom* of the hatch vessel (that is, from underneath the plastic filtrant). This procedure removes large food particles, which helps to reduce the pollutant load.
14. Remove adult brine shrimp with a coarse-mesh net, rinse in tap water of room temperature or slightly cooler, and use as food.

Figure 62 *In preparation for feeding brine shrimp in a rearing vessel, heap approximately 3 tablespoons of finely ground rice bran onto the center of a thick square of cloth.*

15 If necessary, seed the rearing vessels periodically with nauplii.

SEAFOODS

Adequate nutrients are contained in a number of other foods, and live brine shrimp should properly be used as a regular dietary supplement. The most common foods offered by aquarists are pieces of fish, shrimp, scallop, mussel, crab, and other seafoods cut or chopped to appropriate sizes. You should remember four rules. *First, select only seafoods that are relatively lean and not oily*. Appropriate examples are clams, oysters, shrimp, scallops, lobster, crab, flounder, halibut, haddock, and cod. Avoid using salmon, mackerel, herring, tuna, bluefish, or any product that has been breaded or preseasoned. *Second, never use leftovers from a seafood dinner as aquarium food.* Aquarium animals are not like cats and dogs. Cooking additives such as butter, oils, and seasonings might harm them or foul the water. *Third, cook all seafoods by boiling.* Cooking does not lower the nutrient value very much, and the benefit is considerable. Raw seafoods contain numerous bacteria, some pathogenic to marine animals. Heat destroys them. *Fourth, wrap seafoods tightly in plastic wrap and store frozen in plastic freezer bags. Discard seafoods if they float after addition to the aquarium, if they become dry and flaky, or if there are other indications of decline in quality.* There is little point in feeding inferior foods.

GELATIN-BASED FOODS

Marine aquarists are urged to make their own aquarium food in which unflavored gelatin is the *binder* (the substance that holds the other ingredients together). Gelatin-based foods are often superior to seafoods, which can be deficient in lipids and vitamins. The recipe provided here is approximately 6% lipid by weight, excluding any lipids contained in the fresh seafood and vitamin mix.

The recipe is salty because of the clam juice. Salts increase the density of the finished food, ensuring that it sinks. Clam juice

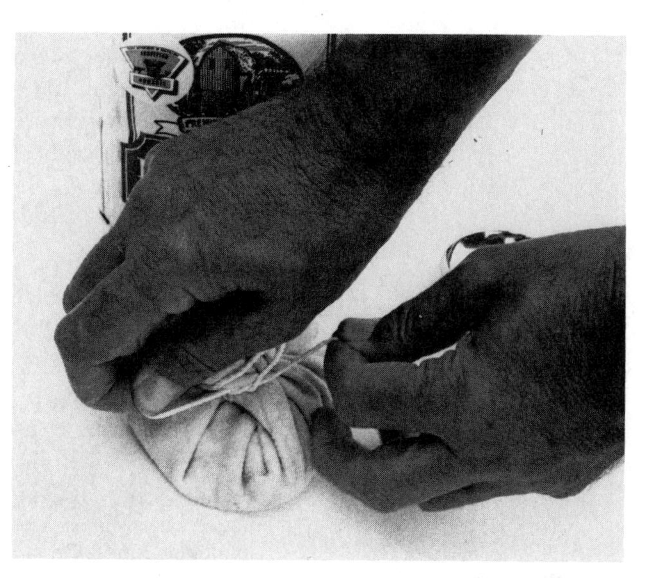

Figure 63 *Fold the cloth to form a tight ball and tie the ends with string.*

also appears to improve palatability. If clam juice is unavailable, substitute an equal volume of new seawater or artificial seawater to retain adequate density. Gelatin-based foods sometimes float if freshwater is substituted. Salty diets are not harmful to marine fishes. They drink seawater continuously, and the invertebrates on which many species feed have tissue fluids comparable with seawater in terms of saltiness. Obviously, high-salt diets are not troublesome to marine invertebrates either.

In addition to gelatin, the principal ingredients are freshly cooked seafoods, whole fish oil (*not* fish liver oil), bottled clam juice, vitamin C tablets (commonly packaged in units of 500 mg), and liquid multivitamins. Whole fish oil is a superior source of long-chain polyunsaturated fatty acids, which marine fishes require. Vitamin C is water soluble and leaches quickly into the environment. Consequently, commercial aquarium foods can be deficient in vitamin C by the time they are ingested. Do not use liquid vitamins intended for infants because they contain artificial flavorings that might reduce palatability of the finished food. Food coloring is optional, although its addition makes uneaten pieces easier to find and remove. I prefer red food coloring, which renders the finished product pink. Whole fish oil and liquid vitamins can be purchased at health food stores. *Refrigerate both products after opening*. Whole fish oils labeled concentrated or *emulsified* are acceptable, although the term *concentrated oil* seems redundant. Ingredients, equipment, and supplies needed to prepare gelatin-based foods are depicted in Figure 64 and listed in Table 11. Consult Tables 12 and 13 for appropriate unit conversions. The procedure can be completed in 15 minutes. A properly made gelatin-based food is firm and slightly rubbery. It should neither crumble nor have the stiff texture of a hockey puck. When placed in seawater or artificial seawater it should sink slowly.

Procedure 17 *How to Make Gelatin-based Food*

1 Boil the seafood (preferably a combination of lean fish, scallops, and unshelled shrimp) for 5 minutes. Remove from the water with a slotted spoon and drain. Do not peel the shrimp, but remove the heads.

2 Weigh 8 oz avdp[15] of freshly boiled seafood on a kitchen scale and transfer to an electric blender. Also add 8 oz fl (1 cup) of

[15]*Avoirdupois weight* is the series of weight units based on the pound of 16 ounces (ounces avoirdupois, symbolized oz avdp). It is important to distinguish the avoirdupois ounce, which must be weighed, from the *fluid ounce* (oz fl), which is determined volumetrically with a measuring cup or similar device. *Weigh* the seafood on a kitchen scale; do not use a measuring cup.

Figure 64 *Ingredients, equipment, and supplies needed to make gelatin-based food for marine aquarium animals (see Table 11). Not shown are paper towels. Product endorsement is not implied.*

TABLE 11 Ingredients, equipment, and supplies for making gelatin-based food; yields approximately 2 lb.

Ingredients	Equipment and Supplies
Bottled clam juice[1] (24 oz fl)[2]	Eggbeater
Food coloring (several drops, optional)	Electric blender
Freshly boiled seafood[3] (8 oz avdp)[2]	Kitchen scale
Liquid vitamins (2 tbsp)	Measuring cup
Unflavored gelatin (2 oz avdp)	Measuring tablespoon
Vitamin C Tablets (500 mg total)	Mixing bowl
Whole fish oil (4 tbsp)	Paper towels
	Pie pan or mold
	Plastic freezer bags
	Plastic wrap
	Pot
	Sauce pan
	Slotted spoon

[1]If unavailable, substitute an equal volume of new seawater or artificial seawater.

[2]Fluid ounces (oz fl) are determined volumetrically with a measuring cup; ounces avoirdupois (oz avdp) are obtained by weighing on a kitchen scale (see text footnote 15).

[3]Preferably a mixture of lean fish (for example, flounder, cod, halibut, or haddock), scallops, and unshelled shrimp.

TABLE 12 English to metric unit conversions with symbols in parentheses.

English Unit	Metric Unit or Standard International Unit Equivalent
Pound (lb)	454 grams (g)
Ounce, avoirdupois (oz avdp)	28.375 grams (g)
Ounce, fluid, U.S. (oz fl)	29.573 milliliters (mL)
Gallon, U.S. (gal)	3.785 liters (L)
Quart, U.S. (qt)	946 milliliters (mL)
Pint, U.S. (pt)	473 milliliters (mL)
Cup	237 milliliters (mL)
Tablespoon (tbsp)	15 milliliters (mL)
Teaspoon (tsp)	5 milliliters (mL)
20 drops	1 milliliter (mL)
Foot (ft)	30.48 centimeters (cm)
Inch (in)	2.54 centimeters (cm)

TABLE 13 English to English unit conversions with symbols in parentheses.

English Unit	Alternate English Equivalent
Pound (lb)	16 ounces, avoirdupois (oz avdp)
Gallon, U.S. (gal)	4 quarts, U.S. (qt)
Quart, U.S. (qt)	2 pints, U.S. (pt)
Cup	8 fluid ounces (oz fl)
	1/2 pint, U.S. (pt)
	16 tablespoons (tbsp)
Tablespoon (tbsp)	1/2 fluid ounce (oz fl)
	3 teaspoons (tsp)
4 tablespoons (tbsp)	1/4 cup
5 1/3 tablespoons (tbsp)	1/3 cup
10 2/3 tablespoons) tbsp)	2/3 cup
12 tablespoons (tbsp)	3/4 cup

bottled clam juice, 4 tablespoons of whole fish oil, 500 mg of vitamin C, 2 tablespoons of liquid vitamins, and several drops of red food coloring. *Shake the whole fish oil and bottled clam juice before pouring*. If clam juice is unavailable, add 8 oz fl (1 cup) of new seawater or artificial seawater. Blend at high speed for 3 minutes.

3 Add 16 oz fl (2 cups) of bottled clam juice to a sauce pan, heat to boiling, and transfer to a mixing bowl. If clam juice is unavailable, substitute an equal volume of new seawater or arti-

ficial seawater. Heat this too, but not to boiling. *The density of freshwater is lower than the densities of seawater and artificial seawaters, and the finished food might float if freshwater is substituted.*

4 Add 2 oz avdp of unflavored gelatin *slowly* to the hot clam juice (alternatively, to the hot seawater or artificial seawater) while mixing *slowly* with an eggbeater. The assistance of another person is helpful. Stir for 3 minutes or until the gelatin dissolves. *Do not use an electric mixer.* Slow mixing is essential to prevent foaming.

5 Add the contents of the blender to the mixing bowl and mix *slowly* with the eggbeater for 3 minutes. *Do not use an electric mixer.* Slow mixing is again essential to prevent foaming.

6 Pour into a pie pan or mold, cover with plastic wrap, and refrigerate.

7 Remove from the refrigerator after gelling occurs. Release from the mold by slicing around the edges with a knife. Blot the surface dry with a paper towel and cut into three pieces. Blotting removes water that has condensed during cooling. Unless removed, it forms a thin layer of ice when the material is frozen. Wrap portions separately in plastic wrap and store frozen in plastic freezer bags.

8 Remove from the freezer immediately before feeding and slice or chop off pieces to appropriate sizes. The pieces occasionally float momentarily before sinking. This is because ice crystals form during freezing. The food sinks slowly as the ice crystals melt.

FEEDING TECHNIQUES

Feeding requirements are summarized in Table 14. However, feeding techniques are important too. Food is almost always available in nature. The inhabitants of coral reefs awake each morning (or evening) to an endless banquet. Signs of starvation and malnutrition are rarely evident. Animals in a marine aquarium can eat only when food is offered; starvation and malnutrition are not rare occurrences.

Overfeeding fouls the water, and every aquarium book admonishes aquarists not to feed too much. This advice is well taken, but not at the expense of starving the animals. *The best technique is to offer small amounts of food several times daily—preferably four times.* Once established, many fishes can exist on two daily feedings, although more are advisable. In nature, planktivores and grazers feed almost continuously during the times they are active. Large carnivores such as groupers and mo-

TABLE 14 Feeding requirements of common groups of marine aquarium fishes and invertebrates.

Animal Group[1]	Food Requirements[2]
Fishes	
Angelfishes (feeding generalists as juveniles)	B_A S G
Angelfishes (pygmy)	{B_A B_N} S G
Basslets	B_A {S G}
Blennies	{B_A B_N} {S G}
Butterflyfishes (feeding generalists)	{B_A B_N} S G
Cardinalfishes	{B_A B_N} S
Damselfishes	{B_A B_N} S G
Dottybacks	{B_A B_N}{S G}
Dragonettes	{B_A B_N}
Drums	S G
Eeltail catfishes	S G
Filefishes	S G
Gobies	{B_A B_N} {S G}
Hawkfishes	B_A {S G}
Jawfishes	B_A B_N
Moorish idol	B_N S G
Morays	S G
Roundheads	S G
Scorpionfishes[3]	S G
Sea basses (anthiines, others)	B_A {S G}
Sea basses (groupers)	S G
Seahorses	{B_A B_N}
Squirrelfishes	S G
Surgeonfishes and tangs	B_A S G
Triggerfishes	S G
Wrasses	B_A {S G}
Invertebrates	
Crustaceans (crabs and shrimps)	{B_A B_N} S G
Sea anemones	B_N{S G}
Sea stars	S G
Sea urchins	S G

[1]Only three foods are necessary to maintain most members of the groups listed.

[2]Codes are B_A (adult brine shrimp), B_N (brine shrimp nauplii), S (seafood), and G (gelatin-based food). Some species might refuse one or more but survive without apparent ill effects. Braces around two foods indicate that either or both may be used, depending on acceptance.

[3]Turkeyfishes require small live fishes (for example, goldfish, guppies, or mollies) once weekly.

rays typically consume considerable amounts of food at a single feeding, then fast for extended periods. Many of these species survive well if fed several times a week.

No specific guidelines can be written for how much food to offer at a feeding. Everything depends on the feeding patterns and competitive interactions of the species maintained. *Never add food to an aquarium and walk away. Always watch the animals while you feed them. Be sure all specimens get enough food and look for signs of weight loss (see Chapter 8).*

When offering brine shrimp (adults or nauplii), follow the transfer techniques described previously in this chapter: (*1*) pour some of the water from the live food container through a *dedicated* net, (*2*) rinse the contents of the net thoroughly in tap water of room temperature or slightly cooler, (*3*) turn the net upside down in the aquarium and allow the brine shrimp to drift free. Afterward, replace at least some of the water lost from the live food container with new seawater or artificial seawater. Do not add more brine shrimp than can be consumed quickly. This takes approximately 10 minutes when adult brine shrimp are used and 30 minutes for nauplii. Brine shrimp nauplii swim with a jerky motion. They can be seen by looking through one end of the aquarium, preferably with a lamp or window in the background.

When offering seafood or gelatin-based food, cut and chop the pieces to appropriate sizes (large pieces for large specimens, small pieces for small ones). This is easier when the food is frozen. Stand in front of the aquarium and drop in small amounts of food from the from the end of the knife. Immersing the knife in the aquarium is not a good idea if some of the animals are aggressive feeders. For convenience, place the food on a small cutting board that you can hold in one hand. Feed aggressive specimens until their interest wanes, then concentrate on the timid ones. Do not stop until all specimens have received enough food. With patience and experience you can feed all animals in a community aquarium adequately in 10 minutes without leaving any food on the bottom.

Marine aquarium animals can be maintained in a good nutritional state for years on combinations of live brine shrimp, cooked seafood, and gelatin-based food. A sample schedule might be: 8:00 a.m.—brine shrimp (adults and nauplii), 12:00 p.m.—gelatin-based food, 4:00 p.m.—seafood, 7:00 p.m.—brine shrimp (adults). Brine shrimp nauplii are necessary only if the aquarium contains sea anemones or small fishes (especially planktivores) less than 2 inches long. Obviously, many aquarists work and are not at home during the day. As mentioned previously, two daily feedings are adequate, so long as the needs of the animals can be satisfied.

FEEDING IDIOSYNCRASIES

I had a childhood friend who ate apples while hanging by his knees from a tree limb. The rest of us would watch eagerly, hoping to see him choke, but he never did. One day his mother asked him to explain this unusual behavior, and he replied that apples tasted better when he was upside down.

The feeding patterns of many marine animals, which are no less odd, tend to become even more idiosyncratic as time passes. Some aquarium specimens seem to prefer the competitive melee of a feeding session; others shun competition and will eat only if given individual attention. Part of this behavior is attributable to species differences, but not all of it. *Avoid repetitive feeding practices because the behavioral repertoires of aquarium animals are dynamic, not static.* In people and animals alike, eating is a far richer experience than the simple act of ingestion. Offering a variety of foods encourages shy animals to eat more consistently and sometimes discourages aggressive aquarium-mates from consuming more than their share. Not infrequently, shy eaters can be helped by including an extra feeding; alternatively, try changing the daily feeding schedule.

Many aquarium animals have been programmed by evolution to operate on schedules different from ours. Successful aquarists take the trouble to learn the habits of animals in their care. Cardinalfishes, for example, are nocturnal predators. They emerge from their shelter spaces in the coral at dusk to feed on tiny animals in the night plankton. Captive cardinalfishes sometimes hide during feedings. Many species can be conditioned to feed in daylight hours but often fare better if brine shrimp nauplii are added just before the lights are turned out.

Most fishes eventually learn to approach the front glass at feeding time. Many can recognize the people who feed them. If fed on a schedule, some aquarium animals become restless as feeding time approaches. Aggressive individuals often chase less dominant members of the community. Vocal fishes such as the emperor angelfish emit irritable grunts that are sometimes loud enough to be heard in the next room. Crabs and shrimps emerge from hiding and scuttle across the bottom. Some animals eat their fill and retire promptly to shelter spaces or swim about disinterestedly. Others remain at the front glass even when satiated, preventing others from eating. Get to know the inhabitants of your aquarium as individuals, just as you would a group of cats or dogs.

CHAPTER

12 Health and Disease

Synopsis *Infectious diseases constitute the principal problem in marine aquarium keeping. Antibacterial agents often kill filter bacteria and can only be used in the treatment aquarium. Never use copper compounds. Copper is toxic to fishes, remains on carbonate gravel surfaces, and is of doubtful effectiveness. Fishes respond physiologically to stress factors, and one response is immune suppression. Stressed fishes are more susceptible to infectious diseases. Proper aquarium management includes minimizing stress responses by controlling stress factors. Perhaps the most stressful practice is chasing a fish, capturing it with a net, and lifting it out of the water. Capture fishes in plastic bags; use nets only for removing dead animals, dead plants, detritus, and uneaten food. A fish's mucus and skin are its first line of defense against pathogenic bacteria. Violation of the skin renders fishes vulnerable to bacterial infections. Transfer fishes with bacterial diseases to the treatment aquarium. Treat for 15 minutes with nifurpirinol (2 mg/L), 12 hours with oxolinic acid (3 mg/L), or 6 hours with a soluble antibacterial agent from the home medicine cabinet (25 mg/L). Treatments exceeding 12 hours are unnecessarily stressful and not recommended. Amyloodinium disease is probably the deadliest disease likely to be encountered in a marine aquarium. An effective cure has not been devised. Destroy all animals and plants in a diseased exhibit or quarantine aquarium, sterilize everything with Clorox®, and condition the subgravel filter again. Treat white-spot disease directly in a diseased exhibit or quarantine aquarium by lowering the specific gravity to approximately 1.012 for 6 days. Alternatively, raise the specific gravity to approximately 1.040 and treat all animals and plants in the treatment aquarium for 15 minutes; treat the diseased exhibit or quarantine aquarium, now devoid of inhabitants, for 30 min-*

utes. Treat worm-infested fishes in the treatment aquarium with praziquantel (10 mg/L for 3 hours) and quarantine for 3 weeks. Sterilize the infested exhibit or quarantine aquarium with Clorox®. Do not treat invertebrates and plants. After removing all invertebrates, treat fish louse infestations directly in the diseased exhibit or quarantine aquarium with trichlorfon at 0.25 to 1.0 mg/L; repeat at 7 and 14 days.

Infectious diseases constitute the principal problem in marine aquarium keeping. I can think of five failings on the part of aquarists that cause this statement to be true. First is failure to recognize and reject sick and injured specimens in a dealer's aquariums (see Chapter 8). The chances of success are much greater if healthy animals are selected. Second is failure to follow established quarantine procedures (see Chapter 7). Diseases are difficult to control if the water and animals are infected from the start. Third is failure to avoid situations and procedures that cause injury to captive animals or lower their resistance to infectious diseases. Fourth is failure to recognize specific diseases and treat them effectively. In my experience, aquarists who can overcome the difficulties inherent in failings 1 through 3 are seldom faced with the fourth. *The survivorship of captive animals is extended more effectively by disease prevention than by disease treatment.* Fifth is treating diseased fishes directly in the exhibit and quarantine aquariums. If the treatment aquarium is too small, buckets and other containers are suitable substitutes. *Diseased animals should be treated only in the treatment aquarium, unless the method of treatment is harmless to the filter bacteria or does not cause other undesirable effects.*

Compounds commonly used to treat diseases can kill beneficial filter bacteria or exert other undesirable effects. Copper compounds, for example, have a dubious capacity to effect cures in diseased fishes, for at least two reasons. First, copper is toxic to both fishes and the disease organisms it is intended to eliminate. The effect, in other words, is nonspecific. Second, copper compounds react chemically with carbonate minerals and bind to their surfaces. Because copper remains on the gravel after treatment has stopped, copper ions are released slowly back into the water for long periods of time.

Eradication of persistent diseases often involves sterilizing the exhibit or quarantine aquarium in which it appeared. Afterward, the subgravel filter must once again be conditioned before the aquarium is capable of sustaining life. This presents a serious situation when diseases appear in the exhibit aquarium. During the conditioning process the animals and plants must be housed elsewhere, and a 20-gal quarantine aquarium is inadequate. If newly acquired animals die of an infectious disease in the quarantine aquarium, sterilize it and start conditioning the subgravel filter immediately. *Always try to keep the subgravel filter of the quarantine aquarium conditioned and the aquarium fully operational for emergencies that might arise in the exhibit aquarium. The filter of the quarantine aquarium can be kept functional by adding an occasional pinch of ammonium salt or a few drops of ammonium salt solution (see Chapter 6).*

STRESS RESPONSES AND STRESS FACTORS

Most of us understand stress from a personal perspective. Being stuck in traffic and late for a meeting elicits certain behavioral responses, including nervousness and irritability. These are expressions of transient physiological changes that immediately preceded them.

Measurable stress responses at the physiological level are numerous. They include abrupt increases in blood cortisol (a steroid hormone), epinephrine (also called adrenaline), which is an amine hormone, and blood sugar (initiated by the rise in cortisol and epinephrine). All decline gradually toward normal values when the stress factor is removed. Stress can therefore be considered in terms of *stress responses* (physiological and behavioral) and the *stress factors* that elicit them. Stress responses, when prolonged, have debilitating consequences, among which is reduced immunity to infectious diseases.

The physiological responses of fishes and other vertebrates to stressful situations are similar to those we experience. The responses of invertebrates are less well known. *Proper aquarium management includes minimizing the incidence and degree of stress responses by controlling the stress factors that elicit them.* Several aquarium practices are confirmed stress factors in fishes, as demonstrated by associated physiological stress responses.

Perhaps the most stressful practice is chasing a fish, capturing it with a net, and lifting it out of the water (Table 15). In fishes subjected to this procedure, the blood cortisol concentration rises immediately, followed quickly by an increase in the concentration of blood sugar. Similar responses have been demonstrated experimentally in fishes confined in small spaces or exposed to social stresses. The same responses occur after abrupt changes in the temperature or specific gravity of the water, when water quality is poor, and in the presence of toxic compounds.

TABLE 15 Factors known to induce physiological stress responses in fishes.

Aquarium Practices
Chasing, as with a with a net
Confinement in a small space that restricts movement
Prolonged chasing prior to capture
Prolonged struggling in a net after capture
Removal from the water
Social Factors
Aggression within (intraspecific) and between (interspecific) species
Crowding
Insufficient number of shelter spaces
Environmental Factors
Abrupt transfer to higher or lower specific gravity
Abrupt transfer to higher or lower temperature
Exposure to ammonia, copper, formalin, chlorine, or ozone
Exposure to low concentrations of dissolved oxygen
Exposure to low pH

Source: Modified from S. Spotte, *Captive Seawater Fishes: Science and Technology,* John Wiley & Sons, Inc., © 1992, reprinted with permission.

Never expose a fish to the air even momentarily. Lifting a fish out of the water causes its gills (Figure 65) to collapse, resulting in brief *hypoxia* (insufficient oxygen) that is followed quickly by measurable physiological stress responses. *When fishes are captured and transferred, always use a plastic bag filled with water, never a net. Restrict the use of nets to removing dead animals, dead plants, detritus, and uneaten food. Insist that the dealer use a plastic bag instead of a net when capturing a fish you have just purchased.*

In experimental studies, fishes injected with cortisol, which mimics some effects of prolonged stress, have lower immunity and contract infectious diseases more readily than control fishes that have not been injected. *The application of stress factors predisposes captive fishes to infectious diseases by lowering their immunity.*

MUCUS AND SKIN

A fish's mucus and skin are its first line of defense against pathogenic bacteria. Fish mucus contains immunity factors in addition to forming a protective physical barrier (Figure 66). Removing

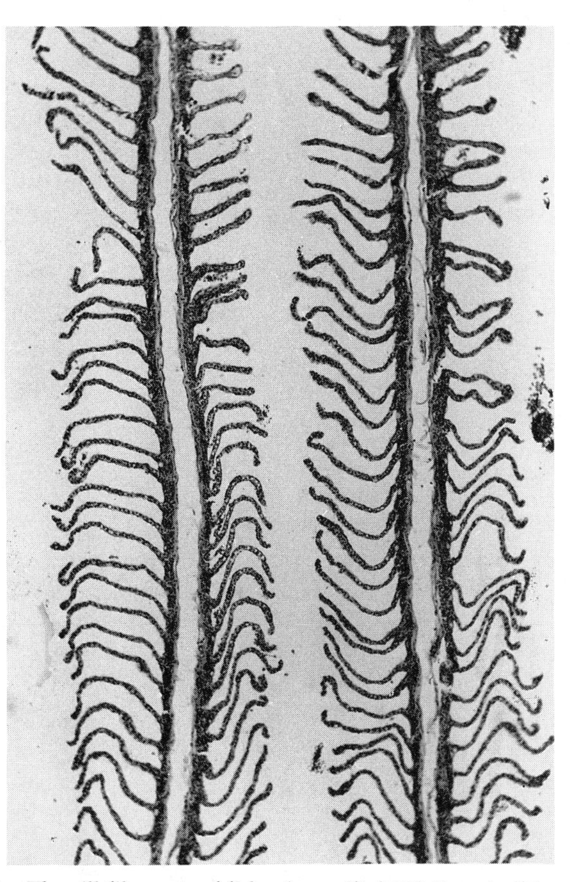

Figure 65 *The gill filaments of fishes (magnified 100 times in this exposure) are delicate and sensitive. Lifting a fish out of water can damage them. Fishes should always be captured and transferred in water-filled plastic bags.* Source: Richard E. Wolke, Marine Pathology Laboratory, The University of Rhode Island.

surface mucus or damaging the mucous cells of the skin compromises any inherent capacity to ward off potentially harmful bacteria. So do cuts, abrasions, punctures, and other violations of the skin's integrity (Figure 67). *The most common cause of injury is chasing a fish and causing it to bump into objects in the aquarium, followed by capture with a net.* Nets strip away mucus, rip fins, break fin rays, damage scales, and inflict cuts and abrasions. *Any violation of the mucus and skin—however small—is a potential site for invasion by pathogenic bacteria.* Once invasion occurs, infections become *systemic*, spreading by means of the circulatory system to the internal organs. Systemic infections are likely to result in death. If fishes must be transferred, plan the capture beforehand

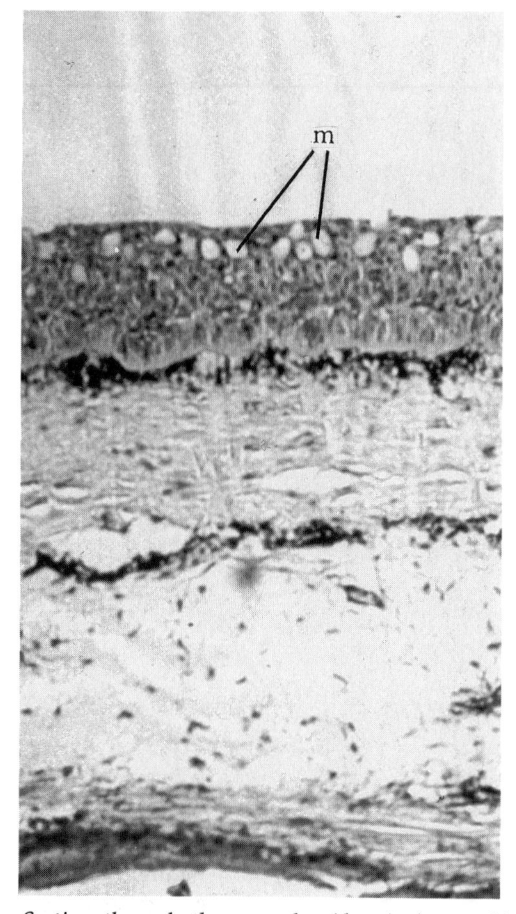

Figure 66 *Section through the normal epidermis (outer skin layer) of a healthy fish (magnified 250 times). m = mucous cells that produce the protective layer of mucus.* Source: Richard E. Wolke, Marine Pathology Laboratory, The University of Rhode Island.

and take steps to accomplish it quickly and without injury by removing some of the aquarium decorations.

INFECTIONS AND INFESTATIONS

Microorganisms, including bacteria and *protozoans* (single-celled animals), cause *infections*. Parasitic worms and crustaceans, which are much larger and multicellular, induce *infestations*. In marine aquariums, bacteria and protozoans are the most troublesome organisms by far. Remedies sold by dealers are of questionable effectiveness, a situation that often forces aquarists to concoct their own.

BACTERIAL DISEASES

In hospitals, bacteria isolated from patients are subjected to *sensitivity testing*, a series of laboratory procedures designed to determine which *antibacterial agents* (also called *antibiotics*) are of optimal effectiveness. This degree of concern is not extended to captive fishes except occasionally at fish farms. Hobbyists seldom know the identities of pathogenic bacteria in their aquariums or the best means for treating the diseases they cause.

Fishes become diseased and die from numerous species of pathogenic bacteria, but the majority are Gram-negative. In the laboratory, *Gram-negative bacteria* are distinguished by layered cell walls that give a characteristic reaction to certain biological stains. Antibacterial agents with specific effectiveness against Gram-negative bacteria often work best; broad-spectrum compounds are the next best choice. As the name suggests, *broad-*

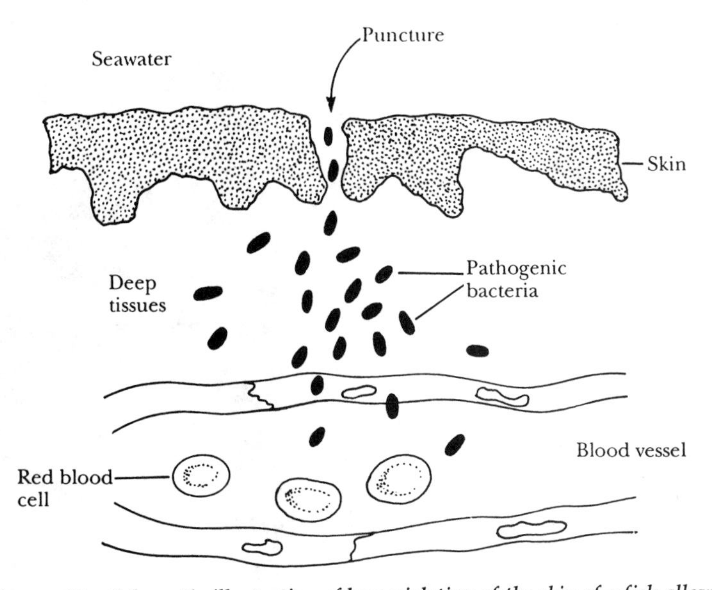

Figure 67 *Schematic illustration of how violation of the skin of a fish allows bacteria to enter the deep tissues and then the circulatory system to produce systemic infections.* Source: Modified from J. A. Bellanti, *Immunology II*, W. B. Saunders Company, © 1971, p. 375, reprinted with permission.

spectrum antibacterial agents are effective against a broad array of bacteria.

A few clinical signs of bacterial diseases in fishes are summarized in Table 16. Only a limited number of antibacterial agents has been licensed in the United States for treating commercially raised fishes and invertebrates. One effective agent is nifurpirinol,[16] sold under the name Prefuran® and formerly available as Furanace® (Figure 68). Another is oxolinic acid, sold as Oxolium® (Figure 69). Knowledgeable dealers should carry both. *Do not apply either product as directed on the labels, because the dosages*

TABLE 16 Some clinical signs of bacterial diseases in marine fishes.

Anorexia (loss of appetite)
Ataxia (loss of coordination)
Discoloration or hemorrhaging of the skin
Emaciation (weight loss)
Fin erosion, which includes loss of tissue from the fin edges
Inactivity, including hovering in corners
Labored breathing
Milky cloudiness of the body surfaces
Open cuts, abrasions, and punctures that do not heal
Persistent, open red sores

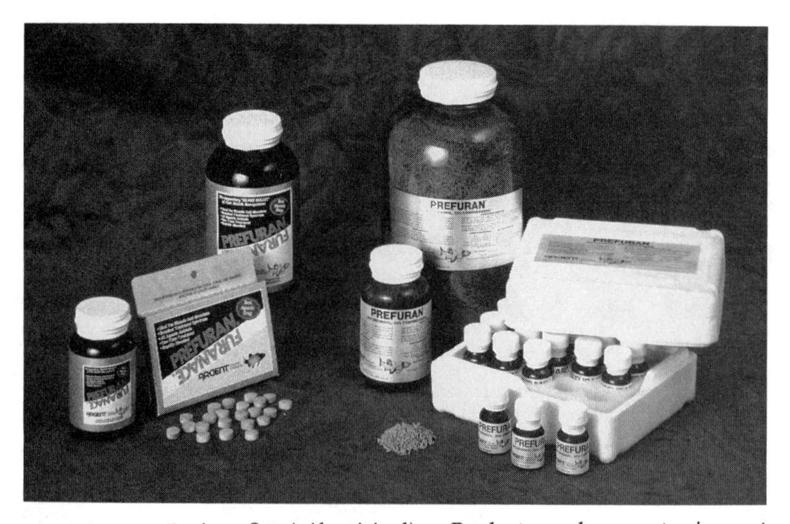

Figure 68 *Prefuran® (nifurpirinol). Product endorsement is not implied.* Source: Argent Chemical Laboratories, 8702 152nd Avenue N.E., Redmond WA 98052.

16Pending approval by the U.S. Food and Drug Administration.

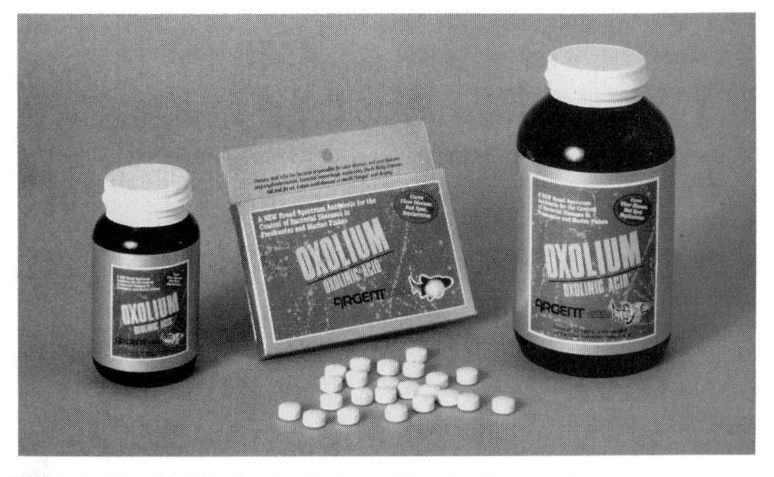

Figure 69 *Oxolium® (oxolinic acid). Product endorsement is not implied.* Source: Argent Chemical Laboratories, 8702 152nd Avenue N.E., Redmond WA 98052.

are too conservative. Dispense as directed in Procedure 18. Antibacterial agents are potentially harmful to filter bacteria; therefore, apply them only in a treatment aquarium. Nifurpirinol can be applied in the treatment aquarium in short baths (for example, 15 minutes) because it is absorbed much more rapidly than oxolinic acid. *Treatments exceeding 12 hours in the treatment aquarium, regardless of the compound used, are unnecessarily stressful and not recommended.*

Procedure 18 ***How to Apply Prefuran® or Oxolium®***

1 Add approximately 9 gal of new seawater or artificial seawater to the treatment aquarium.

2 Drop in a dedicated, weighted air diffuser (see Figure 12) and aerate gently. Add a dedicated immersion heater and adjust the temperature to that of the diseased aquarium. *Dedicated equipment* is equipment used only with a specific aquarium.

3 Select *either* Prefuran® or Oxolium®; do not use both. Tablets of Prefuran® contain 3.8 mg of nifurpirinol. *Use Prefuran® at a final concentration of approximately 2 mg/L of active ingredient.* To achieve this concentration in a final volume of 10 gal (approximately 40 L), 21 tablets are needed. Tablets of Oxolium® each contain 30 mg of oxolinic acid. *Use Oxolium® at a final concentration of approximately 3 mg/L of active ingredient.* To achieve this concentration in a final volume of 10 gal (approximately 40 L), four tablets are needed.

4 Add the appropriate number of Prefuran® or Oxolium® tablets and allow the water to circulate for 30 minutes or until most of the material has dissolved.

5 Capture diseased fishes in plastic bags and transfer them to the treatment aquarium. Addition of a small amount of water is unimportant.

6 Bring the final volume of the treatment aquarium to 10 gal *after* the animals have been added.

7 Treat for 15 minutes (Prefuran®) or 12 hours (Oxolium®).

8 Capture the fishes in plastic bags, but discard part of the water and replace it with water dipped from the quarantine aquarium. Replace the water in the bags *at least* three times, always keeping the fishes submerged completely. *The reason for this step is to prevent remnants of antibacterial agent in the treatment water from killing beneficial bacteria in the subgravel filter of the quarantine aquarium.*

9 When enough water has been changed, release the fishes into the quarantine aquarium (*not* the exhibit aquarium).

10 Unplug the immersion heater, allow it to cool for 5 minutes, and remove it. Empty the water into a sink and rinse the treatment aquarium with tap water.

11 Repeat steps 1 through 10 after 3 days if no improvement is seen.

12 Leave recovering fishes in the quarantine aquarium for at least 2 weeks and look carefully for signs of recurring disease.

13 If all fishes are afflicted, sterilize the diseased aquarium (see Procedure 20).

If neither nifurpirinol nor oxolinic acid is available, consult the household medicine cabinet. Most contain partly empty prescription bottles, each with a few antibacterial tablets or capsules left over from past illnesses. Many of these products can be used for treating fishes with bacterial diseases. Before doing so, keep two factors in mind.

First, if the antibacterial agent is insoluble in water, it cannot be absorbed in therapeutic amounts. The solubilities of common antibacterial agents are given in Table 17. Poor solubility is not necessarily cause for rejection. Marine fishes drink water continuously. In the treatment aquarium the antibacterial agent is ingested along with water and absorbed by the gut. It enters the circulatory system and is transported to diseased tissues and organs. Second, some antibacterial agents are more toxic than others. Observe fishes being treated for labored breathing, loss of

TABLE 17 Solubility in water of common antibacterial agents.

Antibacterial Agent	Good	Fair	Poor
Amoxicillin trihydrate		x	
Cephalosporin C	x		
Chlortetracycline			x
Doxycycline		x(?)[1]	
Erythromycin		x	
Gentamicin	x		
Kanamycin A	x		
Neomycin B hydrochloride		x	
Neomycin B sulfate		x	
Neomycin complex	x		
Oxytetracycline hydrochloride	x		
Penicillin G procaine	x		
Rifampin[2]			x
Streptomycin	x		
Tetracycline trihydrate		x	
Trimethoprim			x

[1]Specific solubility data unavailable.

[2]Rifampin is used to treat fish tuberculosis (mycobacteriosis).

equilibrium, or other signs of toxicity. If not evident before treatment started, these signs probably have been caused by the treatment compound. Move affected fishes immediately to a container of clean seawater or artificial seawater and allow them time to recover. Empty the treatment aquarium, refill it, and try another antibacterial agent.

Procedure 19 *How to Treat Fishes with Antibacterial Agents from the Home Medicine Cabinet*

1. Add approximately 9 gal of new seawater or artificial seawater to the treatment aquarium.
2. Drop in a dedicated, weighted air diffuser (see Figure 12) and aerate gently. Add a dedicated immersion heater and adjust the temperature to that of the diseased aquarium. *Dedicated equipment* is equipment used only with a specific aquarium.
3. Most antibacterial agents formulated for human use contain 250 mg of active ingredient. *Use a final concentration of approximately 25 mg/L of active ingredient.* To achieve this concentration in 10 gal (approximately 40 L), four 250-mg capsules or tablets are needed.
4. Add 1000 mg (1 g) of an antibacterial agent. If the agent is contained in capsules, open them with dry hands and

empty the contents into the water; if in tablet form, crush first. Allow the water to circulate for 30 minutes or until most of the material has dissolved.

5 Capture diseased fishes in plastic bags and transfer them to the treatment aquarium. Addition of a small amount of water is unimportant.

6 Bring the final volume of the treatment aquarium to 10 gal *after* the animals have been added.

7 Treat for 6 hours unless signs of stress are observed.

8 After 6 hours, capture the fishes in plastic bags, but discard part of the water and replace it with water dipped from the quarantine aquarium. Replace the water in the bags *at least* three times, always keeping the fish submerged completely. *The reason for this step is to prevent remnants of antibacterial agent in the treatment water from killing beneficial bacteria in the subgravel filter of the quarantine aquarium.*

9 When enough water has been changed, release the fishes into the quarantine aquarium (*not* the exhibit aquarium).

10 Unplug the immersion heater, allow it to cool for 5 minutes, and remove it. Empty the water into a sink and rinse the treatment aquarium with tap water.

11 Repeat steps 1 through 10 after 3 days if no improvement is seen.

12 Leave recovering fishes in the quarantine aquarium for at least 2 weeks and look carefully for signs of recurring disease.

13 If all fishes are afflicted, sterilize the diseased aquarium (see Procedure 20).

AMYLOODINIUM DISEASE

Amyloodinium disease (also called *velvet disease*), caused by the unicellular organism *Amyloodinium ocellatum*, is probably the deadliest disease likely to be encountered in a marine aquarium. It affects mainly the gills and skin of fishes, although the internal organs are sometimes infected too.

The life cycle of *A. ocellatum* has three stages (Figure 70): (*1*) the *trophont*, or attached parasitic stage (Figure 71); (*2*) the *tomont*, or reproductive stage; and (*3*) the *dinospore* or *tomite*, which swims about searching for a fish to infect and represents the infective stage. All stages are microscopic, although the mass of trophonts in heavy infections imparts a dull, velvety appearance to the skin that is visible without magnification.

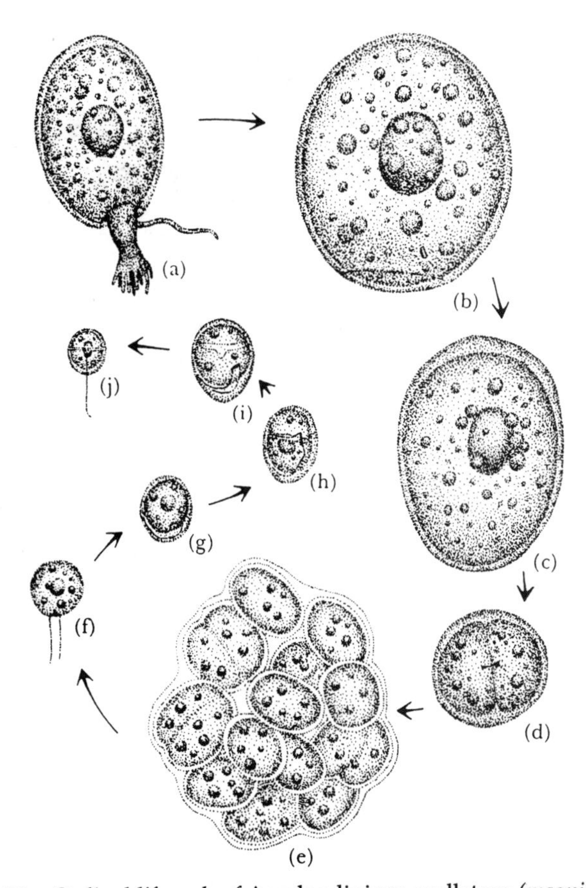

Figure 70 *Stylized life cycle of* Amyloodinium ocellatum *(magnified).* (a) *Trophont, or parasitic stage.* (b,c) *Developing tomont, or reproductive stage.* (d) *Start of cell division in the tomont.* (e) *Continuing cell division in the tomont.* (f-i) *Emergence and further development of dinospores (infective stage).* (j) *Mature dinospore ready to attach to a host fish.* Sources: S. Spotte, *Marine Aquarium Keeping: The Science, Animals, and Art,* John Wiley & Sons, Inc., © 1973, reprinted with permission; modified from R. F. Nigrelli, 1936, *Zoologica* (N.Y.) 21: 129-164 + 9 plates, Osborn Laboratories of Marine Sciences and New York Zoological Society, reprinted with permission.

Diagnosis in the early disease stages is difficult. Some known clinical signs, mostly representative of advanced stages, are summarized in Table 18. An effective cure has not been devised, and diseased fishes seldom survive. *Avoidance by strict prevention is the only reliable control measure.* The most popular treatments include dosing diseased fishes with compounds containing copper. Copper compounds are not recommended for reasons given previously.

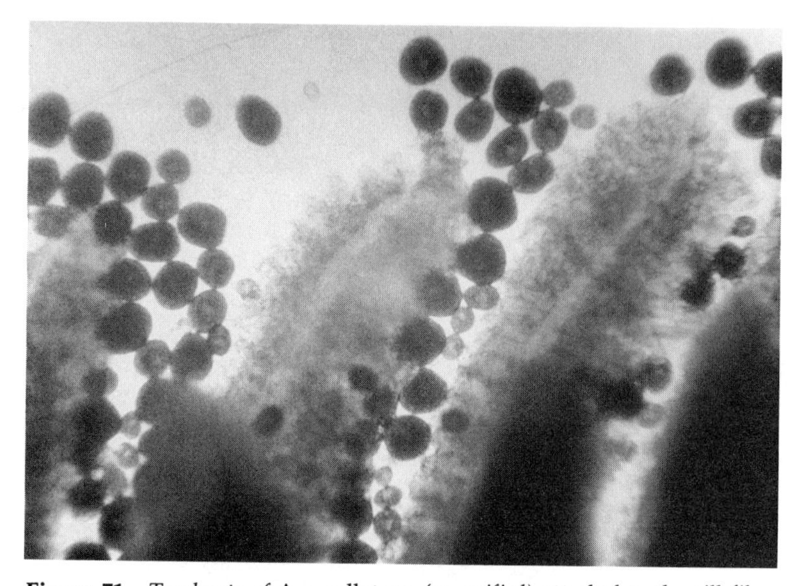

Figure 71 *Trophonts of* A. ocellatum *(magnified) attached to the gill filaments of a lemon peel, a pygmy angelfish. The fish was obtained from a dealer and appeared to be healthy. It died in quarantine. The quarantine aquarium subsequently was sterilized (see Procedure 20), and the disease was never transferred to the exhibit aquarium.* Source: Patricia M. Bubucis, Sea Research Foundation and Marine Sciences Institute, The University of Connecticut.

TABLE 18 Some clinical signs of amyloodinium disease in marine fishes.

Anorexia (loss of appetite)
Gasping or congregating at the surface
Head shaking, indicating infected gills
Scratching against objects in the aquarium
Skin dull, patchy, and velvety
Skin mucus occasionally pinkish
Social species often form tight schools

Antimalarial agents such as quinine hydrochloride and chloroquine are partially effective, sometimes alleviating the most obvious signs of disease and extending survival temporarily. These compounds can be obtained by prescription, although none is a thorough and effective treatment. Transferring diseased fishes to freshwater for 3 minutes causes most of the trophonts to drop off, although a few invariably remain. *Fishes that appear to recover after any attempt at treatment with any compound and by any method are seldom—if ever—free of infection; therefore, they can never be returned to the exhibit aquarium with confidence.*

Inevitably, the result is an outbreak of amyloodinium disease at a later time, perhaps with loss of all fishes in the aquarium.

Once established, amyloodinium disease is persistent and deadly. My advice, harsh as it seems, is to destroy all fishes, invertebrates, and plants in the infected aquarium, sterilize everything with a strong, chlorine-based oxidant such as Clorox®, and start again.

Procedure 20 ***How to Sterilize an Aquarium***

1 Remove all animals and plants and destroy them.

2 Add 1/3 cup of Clorox® per 3 gal of water in the aquarium (the rough equivalent of 10 mL per liter of aquarium water) to yield an approximate 1% Clorox® solution (approximately a 0.0525% hypochloride solution). Pour carefully and wear rubber kitchen gloves. Open the windows to ventilate the room. Let the solution circulate for 6 hours. *If the aquarium is dirty, clean it first; otherwise, much of the oxidizing potential of the Clorox® will be lost to detritus, attached algae, and other organic matter.*

3 To eliminate the chlorine component from the water just treated, add sodium thiosulfate, a chlorine reducing agent, and allow to circulate for 2 hours. Sodium thiosulfate, which is used in film processing, is sold in photography stores as "hypo." Use as a guideline 0.175 g of sodium thiosulfate for each 1 mL of Clorox® applied (that is, 1½ oz avdp per 1½ cups of Clorox® applied). This is the concentration necessary to achieve *neutralization*; in other words, to destroy the oxidizing capacity of the Clorox®.[17] *Commercial dechlorinating agents sold by dealers are too weak to neutralize a 1% solution of Clorox®.*

4 Sterilize all dedicated utensils (for example, buckets, siphon hoses, nets, and scrub pads) in a solution of 1/3 cup of Clorox® to 3 gal of tap water (approximately a 1% Clorox® solution). This the rough equivalent of 10 mL per liter of tap water. Pour carefully and wear rubber kitchen gloves. Soak for 2 hours, then rinse with tap water. Take the aquarium cover outdoors, scrub it with the Clorox® solution, and rinse with tap water.

[17]Clorox® contains 5.25% sodium hypochlorite (NaOCl) by weight. Therefore, 1 L contains 52.5 g of NaOCl. Based on the chemical reaction of sodium thiosulfate ($Na_2S_2O_3 \cdot 5H_2O$) in a chlorinated aqueous solution, 175 g of $Na_2S_2O_3 \cdot 5H_2O$ are needed to neutralize the NaOCl in 1 L of Clorox®. This is the approximate equivalent of 23.3 oz avdp (see text footnote 15) of $Na_2S_2O_3 \cdot 5H_2O$ per gallon of Clorox®.

5 Unplug the immersion heaters and let them cool for 5 minutes. Also unplug the air compressor.
6 Discard the aquarium water, then clean the inside glass surfaces and inside lip with a scrub pad.
7 Remove the airlifts, immersion heaters, and decorations and clean them in a sink with tap water.
8 Add some tap water to the empty aquarium, stir the gravel, and siphon out the water. Be sure to rinse the inside glass surfaces and inside lip. Repeat until the rinse water is not discolored or opaque. *During the life cycle of* A. ocellatum, *reproduction commences when the trophonts detach from diseased fishes, fall to the gravel at the bottom, and become tomonts. Siphoning the gravel reduces their numbers.*
9 Level the gravel, install the airlifts and immersion heaters, and set the decorations in place.
10 Refill the aquarium with new seawater or artificial seawater, plug in the immersion heaters and air compressor, and set the aquarium cover in place.
11 Start conditioning the subgravel filter (see Chapter 6).

WHITE-SPOT DISEASE

White-spot disease of fishes (also called *cryptocaryoniasis* and *saltwater "ich"*) is caused by the ciliate protozoan *Cryptocaryon irritans*. The organism's life cycle is illustrated in Figure 72. Like *Amyloodinium ocellatum*, it has three stages, although the two parasites are unrelated. Parasitic *trophonts* infect the skin, gills, and occasionally the eyes of fishes. The reproductive stage is the *tomont*. *Tomites* represent the free-swimming, infective stage. The trophonts are larger than those of *Amyloodinium ocellatum*. They move about slowly, ingesting blood and cellular material and causing extensive damage. A trophont eventually stops feeding, changes into a tomont, and falls to the bottom. After undergoing cell division, as many as 200 tomites hatch and immediately seek a fish to infect.

Clinical signs are summarized in Table 19. Two effective treatments are to lower the specific gravity to approximately 1.012 for 6 days or raise it to approximately 1.040 for 15 minutes, both from a starting range of 1.023 to 1.025 at 80°F. Success depends partly on whether the animals subjected to either procedure can survive a change this abrupt and extreme. Induction of stress is inevitable, but the risk is worthwhile if the treatment works. *Invertebrates and plants should be treated along with the diseased fishes because they might harbor the parasites on their surfaces.*

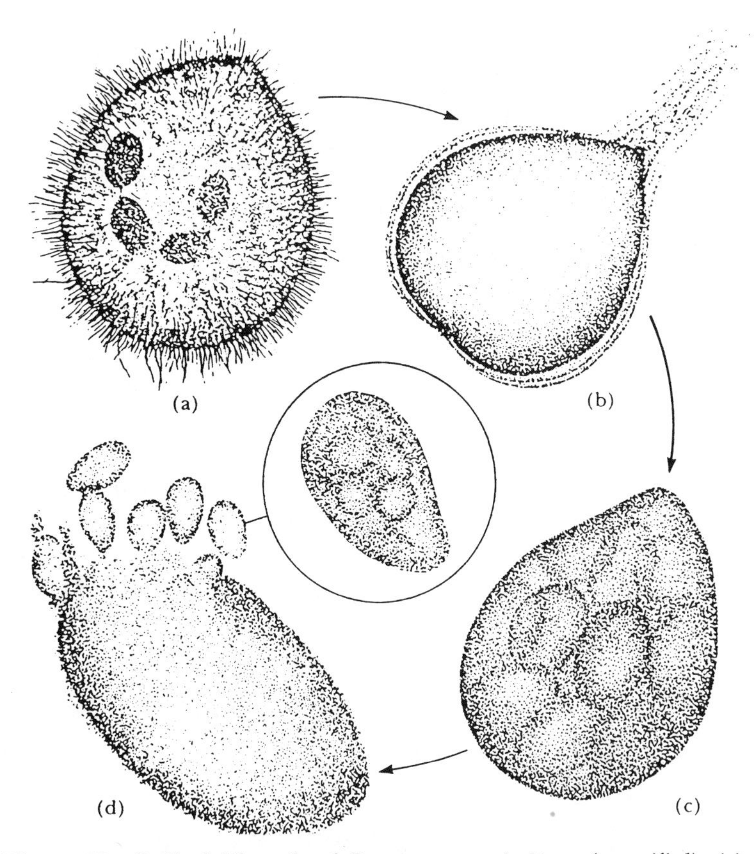

Figure 72 *Stylized life cycle of* Cryptocaryon irritans *(magnified).* (a) *Trophont, or parasitic stage.* (b) *Tomont, or reproductive stage.* (c) *Tomont with developing tomites.* (d) *Free-swimming tomites (infective stage) from the ruptured tomont.* Sources: S. Spotte, *Captive Seawater Fishes: Science and Technology,* John Wiley & Sons, Inc., © 1992, reprinted with permission; modified from R. F. Nigrelli and G. D. Ruggieri, 1966, *Zoologica* (N.Y.) 51: 97-102 + 7 plates, Osborn Laboratories of Marine Sciences and New York Zoological Society, reprinted with permission.

TABLE 19 Some clinical signs of white-spot disease in marine fishes.

Anorexia (loss of appetite)
Cloudy corneas
Excessive mucus production
Pale skin
Pinhead-sized white spots on body surfaces
Respiratory distress

Antimalarial agents (for example, quinine hydrochloride and chloroquine) are sometimes effective, although not consistently so. Compounds containing copper are favored by most aquarists, although I disagree strongly with their use under any circumstances for reasons given previously.

Specific gravity manipulation appears to be more effective than copper treatment and much safer. It offers hope of eradicating white-spot disease from exhibit and quarantine aquariums without the need to sterilize everything and start again, as is necessary with amyloodinium disease. *Specific gravity manipulation for treatment of white-spot disease is relatively safe in exhibit and quarantine aquariums.* Biological filtration might be interrupted temporarily, and periodic ammonia determinations are recommended for 3 weeks after the specific gravity has been restored to normal. *If the ammonia concentration increases to dangerously high levels, make partial water changes.*

Specific gravity manipulation is difficult and messy. In the dilution method of treatment (see Procedure 21), 50% of the water from the diseased aquarium is discarded and replaced with freshwater. However, the original specific gravity cannot be restored later simply by removing some of the water and replacing it with full-strength seawater or artificial seawater. The resulting solution will still be too dilute. All the water must be replaced. The concentration method of treatment (see Procedure 22) calls for increasing the specific gravity of the diseased aquarium by addition of artificial sea salts. Afterward, a portion of the treated water is removed and replaced with freshwater to restore the original specific gravity.

Procedure 21 ***How to Treat White-spot Disease by the Dilution Method***

1. Unplug the immersion heaters and air compressor of the diseased exhibit or quarantine aquarium, but leave the animals, plants, and decorations in place.
2. Stir the gravel and discard 50% of the water and as much detritus as possible by siphoning. *During the life cycle of* C. irritans, *reproduction commences when the trophonts detach from diseased fishes, fall to the gravel at the bottom, and become tomonts. Siphoning the gravel reduces their numbers.*
3. Replace the discarded volume with an equal volume of tap water that has been treated with a commercial dechlorinating agent and adjusted to the aquarium temperature.
4. Plug in the immersion heaters and air compressor. Check the specific gravity after 30 minutes. The value should be close to 1.012. Adjust the specific gravity upward as neces-

sary with artificial sea salts or downward with dechlorinated tap water. Allow to circulate for 30 minutes after each small addition and determine the specific gravity again. Circulate for 6 days.

5 Sterilize all dedicated utensils (for example, buckets, siphon hoses, nets, and scrub pads) in a solution of 1/3 cup of Clorox® to 3 gal of tap water (approximately a 1% Clorox® solution). This the rough equivalent of 10 mL per liter of tap water. Pour carefully and wear rubber kitchen gloves. Soak for 2 hours, then rinse with tap water.

6 Take the aquarium cover outdoors, scrub it with the Clorox® solution, rinse with tap water, and place it back on the aquarium.

7 After 6 days, unplug the immersion heaters and air compressor.

8 Capture the animals in plastic bags and transfer them temporarily to dedicated buckets of new seawater or artificial seawater adjusted to the aquarium temperature. Transfer the plants by hand. Aerate mildly with a weighted air diffuser (see Figure 12). *Many marine animals are sensitive to abrupt increases in specific gravity after a prolonged confinement in water of low specific gravity. Potential stress can be ameliorated somewhat by adjusting specific gravity values of the buckets to an intermediate value (for example, 1.018) beforehand and allowing the animals and plants 6 hours to acclimate.*

9 Stir the gravel, then siphon out all the water and as much detritus as possible.

10 Refill with new full-strength (undiluted) seawater or artificial seawater adjusted to the aquarium temperature. Plug in the immersion heaters and air compressor.

11 After 6 hours, remove the animals from the buckets with plastic bags and transfer them to the exhibit aquarium. Transfer the plants by hand.

12 Sterilize all dedicated utensils (repeat step 5), but do not sterilize the aquarium cover again.

Procedure 22 *How to Treat White-spot Disease by the Concentration Method*

1 Add 8 gal of seawater or artificial seawater to the treatment aquarium. Aerate mildly with a weighted air diffuser (see Figure 12). *Do not treat fishes directly in a diseased exhibit or quarantine aquarium by the concentration method because the volume of water is too large for rapid dilution.* If the treatment aquarium is too small to hold all the specimens, distribute

the rest to aerated dedicated buckets, each containing a known volume of new seawater or artificial seawater.

2. During treatment, the final specific gravity should be 1.040 at 80°F. Unfortunately, the amount of artificial sea salts required to achieve this value cannot be calculated exactly, but 4 oz avdp (see text footnote 15) per gallon of water (30 g/L) should be close. Weigh the amounts of artificial sea salts needed to treat the exhibit or quarantine aquarium (whichever is infected), treatment aquarium, and any treatment buckets. Use a kitchen scale and place the batches of weighed salts in separate labeled containers.
3. Dissolve the artificial sea salts allocated for the treatment aquarium and treatment buckets directly in the designated vessels. After the salts have dissolved, check the specific gravity by removing water samples from each treatment vessel and diluting with an equal volume of freshwater. If the concentrated specific gravity is 1.040, the diluted samples should be close to 1.020. Adjust specific gravity upward as necessary with artificial sea salts or downward with tap water that has been treated with a commercial dechlorinating agent. Allow to circulate for 30 minutes after each small addition and determine the specific gravity again.
4. Have a single large container of new seawater or artificial seawater at normal specific gravity ready to receive the animals after treatment. This is the *recovery container*.
5. Stir the gravel of the diseased exhibit aquarium and siphon out 1% of the water. This withdrawal is to compensate for the increase in volume that will occur when artificial sea salts are added to raise the specific gravity.
6. Capture the animals in plastic bags and transfer them *with a minimum amount of water* to the treatment vessels. Transfer the plants by hand.
7. After 15 minutes, capture the animals in plastic bags *with a minimum amount of water* and transfer them quickly to the recovery container. Aerate mildly with a weighted air diffuser.
8. Remove the cover from the diseased exhibit or quarantine aquarium and set it aside. Add the preweighed artificial sea salts to the aquarium and treat for 30 minutes.
9. After 30 minutes, unplug the immersion heaters and air compressor, then siphon and discard 40% of the water along with as much detritus as possible. *During the life cycle of* C. irritans, *reproduction commences when the trophonts detach from diseased fishes, fall to the gravel at the bottom, and become tomonts. Siphoning the gravel reduces their numbers.*

10 Replace the volume lost from the exhibit aquarium with an equal volume of dechlorinated tap water.
11 Plug in the immersion heaters and air compressor, allow the water to circulate for 30 minutes, and determine the specific gravity. Adjust downward as necessary with declorinated tap water. Allow to circulate for 30 minutes after each small addition and determine the specific gravity again.
12 Capture the animals in plastic bags and transfer them *with a minimum amount of water* to the exhibit aquarium.
13 Sterilize all dedicated utensils (for example, buckets, siphon hoses, nets, and scrub pads) in a solution of 1/3 cup of Clorox® to 3 gal of tap water (approximately a 1% Clorox® solution). This the rough equivalent of 10 mL per liter of tap water. Pour carefully and wear rubber kitchen gloves. Soak for 2 hours, then rinse with tap water.
14 Take the aquarium cover outdoors, scrub it with the Clorox® solution, rinse with tap water, and place it back on the aquarium.

PARASITIC WORMS

Cats and dogs become infested by worms that inhabit the digestive tract, heart, lungs, and other internal organs. Fishes are infested by internal worms too, although the most troublesome kinds in aquariums are external, parasitizing the gills and skin (Figure 73).

Infested fishes rub or scratch against objects in the aquarium. If a fish dies, external worm infestations can be confirmed only by examining the gills or skin scrapings under magnification. Parasitic worms are difficult to eradicate, and their eggs, which hatch in the gravel, no less so. The compound praziquantel is an effective treatment. Praziquantel as Droncit® is obtainable by prescription from veterinarians, who use it to treat cats and dogs for internal worm infestations. However, treating a large aquarium with praziquantel is expensive. The easiest procedure is to treat infested fishes in the treatment aquarium, transfer them to the quarantine aquarium, and sterilize the infested exhibit aquarium (see Procedure 20).

Procedure 23 ***How to Treat External Worm Infestations***

1 Add 8 gal of new seawater or artificial seawater to the treatment aquarium. Aerate mildly with a weighted air diffuser (see Figure 12).

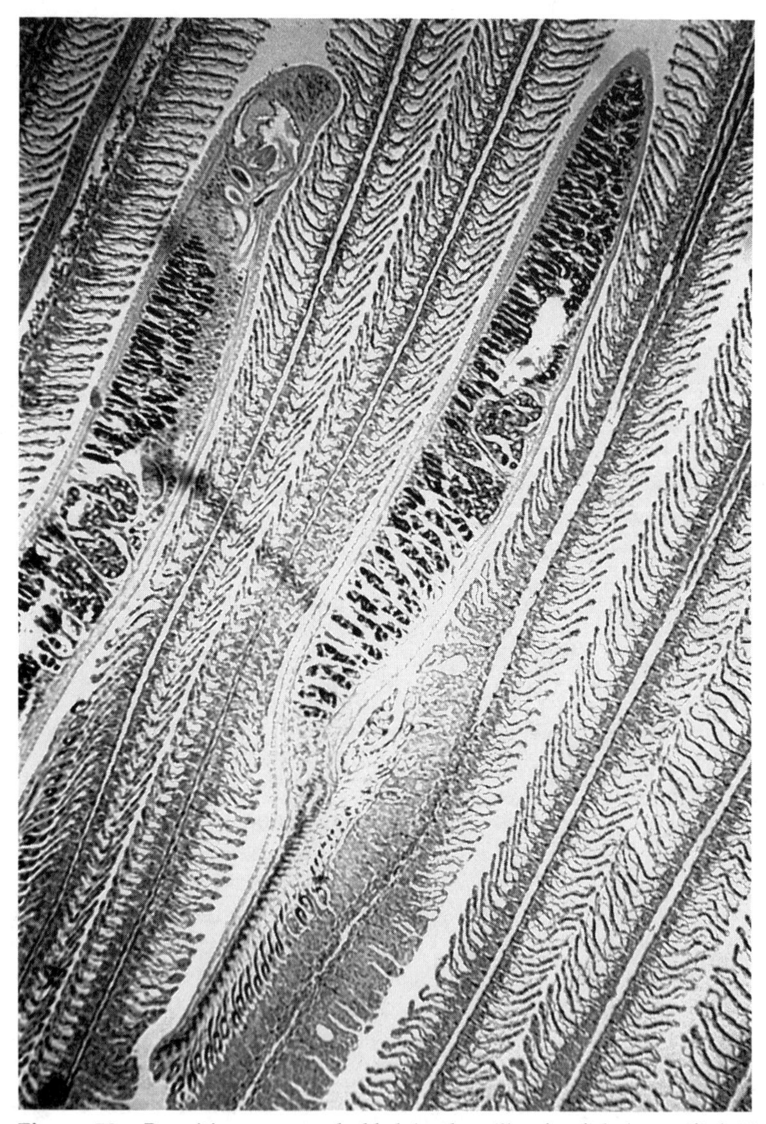

Figure 73 *Parasitic worms embedded in the gills of a fish (magnified 25 times).* Source: Richard E. Wolke, Marine Pathology Laboratory, The University of Rhode Island.

2 Capture the animals in plastic bags and transfer them with a minimum amount of water to the treatment aquarium. If the treatment aquarium is too small to hold all specimens, distribute the rest to buckets of new seawater or artificial seawater, each containing a known volume of water. Aerate mildly with weighted air diffusers.

3 Transfer invertebrates and plants (the latter by hand) to buckets of clean seawater or artificial seawater and aerate mildly with weighted air diffusers. *These organisms will not be treated.*
4 Calculate the amount of praziquantel required to treat each container at an approximate concentration of 10 mg per liter of water. For example, if the tablets available contain 34 mg of active ingredient, each tablet is sufficient to treat approximately 3½ L. Dissolve separate amounts for each container in disposable plastic cups with a little seawater or artificial seawater.
5 Treat for 3 hours, then capture the fishes in plastic bags with a minimum amount of water and transfer them to the quarantine aquarium. Quarantine until the subgravel filter of the exhibit aquarium has been conditioned (approximately 3 weeks, see step 7).
6 Discard the treatment water and sterilize all dedicated utensils (for example, buckets, siphon hoses, nets, and scrub pads) in a solution of ⅓ cup of Clorox® to 3 gal of tap water (approximately a 1% Clorox® solution). This the rough equivalent of 10 mL per liter of tap water. Pour carefully and wear rubber kitchen gloves. Soak for 2 hours, then rinse with tap water.
7 Sterilize the infested aquarium (see Procedure 20), discard the water, and start the conditioning process (see Chapter 6).

FISH LICE

Captive fishes are sometimes acquired with infestations of parasitic crustaceans. These go under the general name of *fish lice*, and they have the potential to cause heavy mortalities. Here the term *fish louse* is limited to a group of parasitic crustaceans called *argulids* (Figure 74), which infest the gills and skin. Many are large enough to be visible without magnification. Argulids lay eggs on the glass, decorations, airlifts, and other stationary objects. Depending on the species, females deposit 20 to 300 eggs. After hatching, the young seek a fish to infest. Argulids feed on the tissues of their hosts, causing extensive damage. Bacteria enter the open wounds, and fishes that are not killed directly by the argulids often die later of bacterial diseases.

Trichlorfon, an insecticide, is effective against fish lice at concentrations of 0.25 to 1 mg per liter of aquarium water, but can be toxic at the higher end of this range. *Sharks, skates, and rays are especially susceptible to trichlorfon toxicity even at low concentrations. So are many invertebrates, notably crustaceans.* Chemically pure

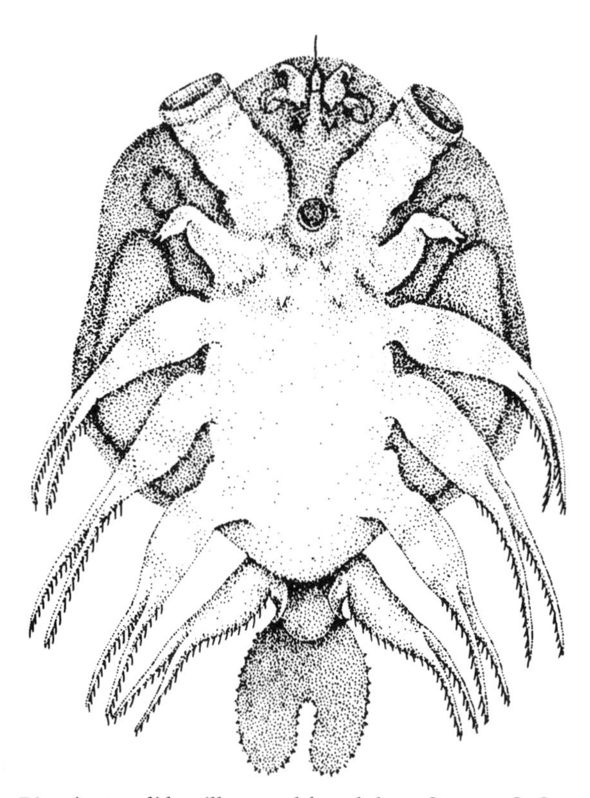

Figure 74 *An argulid as illustrated from below.* Source: S. Spotte, *Marine Aquarium Keeping: The Science, Animals, and Art,* John Wiley & Sons, Inc., © 1973, reprinted with permission.

trichlorfon is not available to amateur marine aquarists. Suppliers ordinarily restrict distribution to licensed research laboratories. Some manufacturers of home aquarium remedies combine trichlorfon with antibacterial agents,[18] which is unfortunate because trichlorfon alone does not harm filter bacteria and can be used to treat infested fishes directly in exhibit and quarantine aquariums after the invertebrates have been removed. If a combined product is used, transfer infested fishes and plants to the treatment aquarium and apply the remedy. Plants might harbor fish louse eggs and should be treated. Place the invertebrates in a separate container of aerated seawater or artificial seawater but do not not treat them. Sterilize the infested aquarium (see Procedure 20) and start the conditioning process.

[18]Manufacturers of home aquarium remedies sometimes list only the generic name of trichlorfon, which is (2,2,2-trichloro-1-hydroxyethyl)-phosphonic acid dimethyl ester.

Trichloracide® (Figure 75) contains only trichlorfon as the active ingredient. At 0.24 mg/L, the trichlorfon concentration is at the low end of the recommended dosage range and therefore conservative. Refer to Procedure 24 if Trichloracide® is used to treat fish louse infestations. If the infestations occur at an aquaculture installation or similar facility that has a licensed laboratory, Procedure 25 can be substituted to dispense generic trichlorfon.[19] With either procedure, vary the trichlorfon concentration according to the known or suspected sensitivities of the parasite and hosts. For example, double the dosage in Procedure 24 to attain an approximate concentration of 0.5 mg/L of trichlorfon; conversely, halve the concentration in Procedure 25 if the situation calls for an approximate dosage of 0.25 mg/L. *Procedures 24 and 25 can also be used to treat external worm infestations if praziquantel is unavailable.*

Procedure 24 ***How to Use Trichloracide® at 0.24 mg/L***

1 Transfer all invertebrates to the quarantine aquarium. Leave fishes and plants in the infested exhibit aquarium.

2 In a disposable paper cup dissolve 1/4 teaspoon of Trichloracide® powder for each 200 L (approximately 50 gal) of aquar-

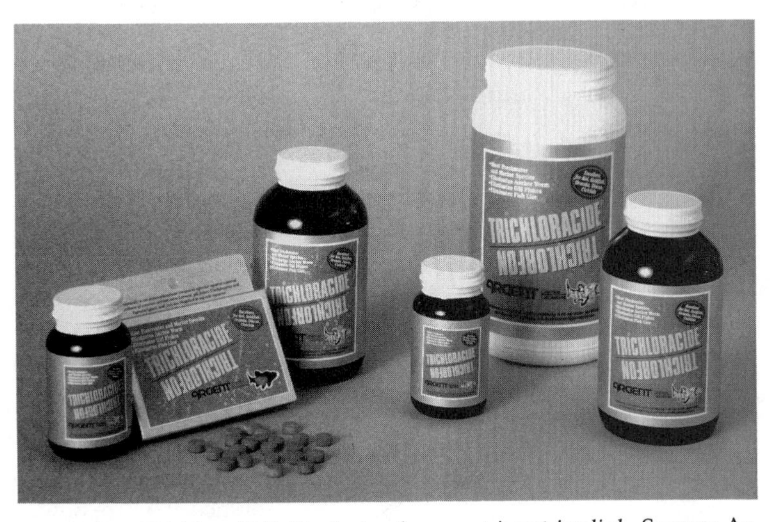

Figure 75 *Trichloracide®. Product endorsement is not implied.* Source: Argent Chemical Laboratories, 8702 152nd Avenue N. E., Redmond WA 98052.

[19]One supplier of generic trichlorfon is Sigma Chemical Company, P.O. Box 14508, St. Louis MO 63178.

ium water. Alternatively, dissolve 1 Trichloracide® tablet for each 40 L (approximately 10 gal) of aquarium water. Knowledgeable dealers should stock Trichloracide® tablets.

3 Add the contents of the cup to the infested aquarium. Ignore any undissolved material, which is the vehicle or carrier. The active ingredient leaches rapidly into the water.

4 Trichlorfon in aqueous solutions degrades gradually with time. Repeat the treatment after 7 and 14 days to kill newly hatched argulids.

5 Wait an additional 7 days, then discard 50% of the water and replace it with new seawater or artificial seawater. While performing this step, stir the gravel and siphon out as much detritus as possible.

6 Wait another 3 days before returning the invertebrates.

Procedure 25 ***How to Make and Dispense Concentrated Trichlorfon Solution to Attain 0.5 mg/L (Licensed Laboratories Only)***

1 Make a concentrated trichlorfon solution by dissolving 5 g in a little distilled water and bringing the volume to 1 L with distilled water. Cap the top with Parafilm® or waxed paper, hold tightly, and shake to dissolve. If possible, use a 1-L volumetric flask to perform this step. *Accuracy is important because trichlorfon to treat the infested exhibit aquarium will be dispensed directly from this concentrated solution.*

2 Each milliliter of concentrated solution contains 5 mg of trichlorfon. *To treat at a dosage of 0.5 mg/L, dispense 1 mL per 10 L of aquarium water.*

3 Before treating, transfer all invertebrates to a quarantine aquarium. Leave the fishes and plants in the infested exhibit aquarium.

4 Consult step 2 and add the appropriate volume of concentrated trichlorfon solution directly to the infested exhibit aquarium (see Tables 12 and 13 for equivalent measures).

5 Repeat the addition after 7 and 14 days to kill newly hatched argulids.

6 Wait an additional 7 days, then discard 50% of the water and replace it with new seawater or artificial seawater. While performing this step, stir the gravel and siphon out as much detritus as possible.

7 Wait another 3 days before returning the invertebrates.

8 *Example 1:* For an aquarium containing 40 gal of water,

$$40\,\text{gal} \times \frac{3.785\,\text{L}}{1\,\text{gal}} = 151\,\text{L}.$$

9 Ask the question, If 1 mL of concentrated trichlorfon solution treats 10 L, how many milliliters are required to treat 151 L? Find the answer by setting up a simple proportion, cross multiplying, and solving for x. Notice that liters cancel out and milliliters, the units of expression of x, are included in x:

$$\frac{1\,\text{mL}}{10\,\text{L}} = \frac{x}{151\,\text{L}}$$

$$(10\,\text{L})(x) = 151\,\text{L}$$

$$x = \frac{151\,\cancel{\text{L}}}{10\,\cancel{\text{L}}}$$

$$x = 15\,\text{mL}.$$

10 *Example 2:* Alternatively, state the objective, which is to dispense 0.5 mg of trichlorfon per liter of aquarium water from a concentrated solution in which each liter contains 5000 mg (i.e., 5 g) of trichlorfon. Therefore,

$$\left(\frac{0.5\,\cancel{\text{mg}}\ \text{tri}\cancel{\text{chl}}\text{orfon}}{\cancel{1\text{L}}\ \text{aqua}\cancel{\text{ri}}\text{um}\ \text{w}\cancel{\text{a}}\text{ter}}\right)\left(\frac{\cancel{1\text{L}}\ \text{trichlorfon}}{5000\,\cancel{\text{mg}}\ \text{trichl}\cancel{\text{o}}\text{rfon}}\right)\left(\frac{150\,\text{L}\ \text{aqua}\cancel{\text{ri}}\text{um}\ \text{w}\cancel{\text{a}}\text{ter}}{1}\right)$$

$$= \frac{0.5\,\text{L trichlorfon}}{5000}$$

$$= 0.015\,\text{L}$$

$$= 15\,\text{mL}.$$

CHAPTER

13 Communal Living

Synopsis *When selecting animals for the aquarium you must consider the social aspects. This is especially important when choosing fishes. Territorial fishes fare poorly if too many individuals are crowded into a small space. Home-ranging fishes roam throughout a large area. Many have active life styles that make them unsuited to aquarium living. Solitary fishes prefer solitude, shunning others of their species and often behaving aggressively toward them. Conversely, schooling as a social behavior is impossible to express when individuals are kept alone. Cryptic fishes—those that hide or use camouflage techniques to make themselves difficult to see—are stressed unduly in aquariums devoid of caves, crevices, or a proper substratum. Sea anemones are mostly solitary, although some species clump together in nature. Sea urchins retire to individual shelter spaces during the day and emerge at night to feed on algae. Most shrimps and crabs maintained in marine aquariums do not warrant special consideration in terms of social requirements. All animals must have access to shelter spaces where they can take refuge from aggression or simply spend the night.*

A marine aquarium is a closed society. None of the inhabitants can leave without the aquarist's decree, nor do any have a choice of companionship. The temptation is to view aquarium animals simply as living ornaments, although this does them a disservice. In fact, their social lives are intricate and varied, and each species has its special requirements. When selecting animals for the aquarium—and maintaining them afterward—you must consider the social aspects. This is especially important when choosing fishes.

Territorial fishes (those that defend a particular location against intrusion) fare poorly if too many individuals are crowded into a small space. *Home-ranging* fishes roam throughout a large area. Many have active life styles that make them unsuited to aquarium living. *Solitary* fishes prefer solitude, shunning others of their species and often behaving aggressively toward them. Conversely, of all known fish species (estimated to be perhaps 20,000) approximately 25% are gregarious and form schools at some time in their lives. Schooling as a social behavior is impossible to express when individuals are kept alone. *Cryptic* fishes (those that hide or use camouflage techniques to make themselves difficult to see) are stressed unduly in aquariums devoid of caves, crevices, or a proper substratum. As emphasized in Chapter 9, all aquarium animals must have access to shelter spaces where they can take refuge from aggression or simply spend the night.

TERRITORIAL FISHES

Territorial fishes defend a fixed location against their own or other species. The interior of the territory includes a shelter space into which the defender retreats if threatened by an aggressor too large to chase away (Figure 76). The shelter space is also used during the night. A territory has invisible boundaries that are guarded avidly against encroachment. Territories often shrink to accommodate population increases and expand during times when the population becomes depleted. Ecologists disagree on whether "optimal" territory sizes exist for any species of animal.

Some damselfishes are among the most aggressively territorial of marine aquarium fishes. In crowded aquariums, several damselfishes might divide all the space among themselves just as they would in nature (Figure 77). Such a situation causes endless strife as less aggressive individuals are chased back and fourth across territorial boundaries. When planning a community aquarium, consider that the presence of too many aggressively territorial fishes is disruptive.

Other territorial fishes are peaceful most of the time, demonstrating only mild incidences of intraspecific (within species) aggression. Jawfishes, which often live in colonies, belong in this category. Jawfishes dig burrows in the substratum, which are used as shelter spaces at night. They need at least 3 inches of mixed coral hash, coral gravel, and coral rubble (see Table 2 and Figure 24; coral rubble is not depicted). Gravels and rubble of

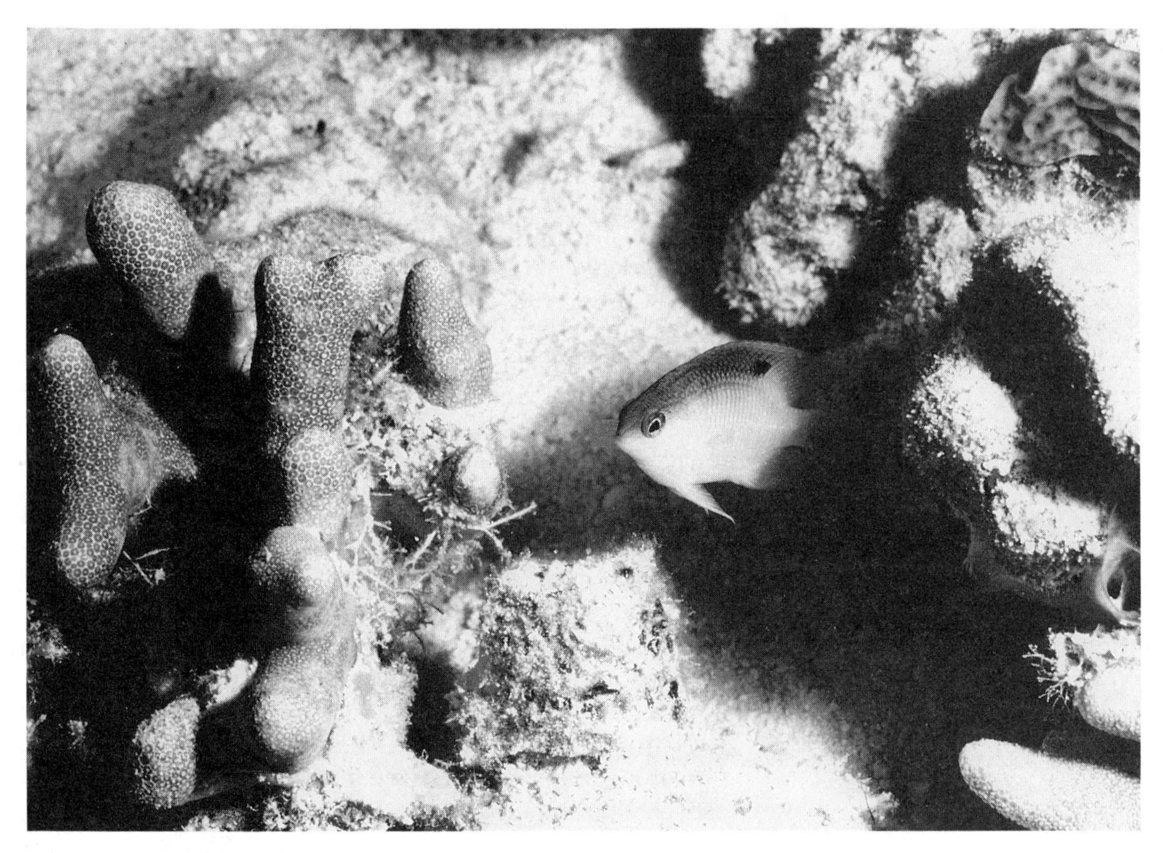

Figure 76 *The beaugregory* (Pomacentrus leucostictus) *is territorial (also see Color Plate 4c). This juvenile specimen is backing into the shelter space inside its territory. Photographed at Ambergris Cay, Belize, Central America, 15 feet.*

Figure 77 *These juvenile threespot damselfish have divided the space over a large coral head among themselves. Territorial boundaries are invisible to a diver but known intimately to the fish, which defend them vigorously (also see Color Plate 4d). Photographed at Bonaire, Netherlands Antilles, 45 feet.*

different sizes are necessary for reinforcing the walls of burrows to keep them from collapsing.

HOME-RANGING FISHES

Many fishes that do not defend territories nonetheless have home ranges. A *home range* is an area that is not defended, although all feeding, reproduction, and sheltering occurs within its boundaries. Home ranges can be large, sometimes extending more than a mile. Many home-ranging species are grazers, feeding on algae and sponges. Still others are planktivores. Most are peaceful. Many are active, unable to adjust to the confinement of aquariums except when juveniles. Notable in this group are the surgeonfishes and tangs (Figure 78), wrasses, parrotfishes, grunts, and snappers. Wrasses typically burrow into the substratum at dusk and do not emerge until well after daylight. Aquariums with wrasses should have at least 3 inches of loose filtrant, preferably coral hash (see Table 2 and Figure 24b). If the gravel is too coarse, too shallow, or both, wrasses experience difficulty when attempting to burrow.

Figure 78 *Blue tangs* (Acanthurus coeruleus) *often cruise coral reefs in large schools, pausing intermittently to feed on algae attached to dead coral (also see Color Plate 10c). Photographed at Key Largo, Florida, 30 feet.*

SOLITARY FISHES

Most angelfishes, filefishes, and morays (Figure 79) lead solitary lives, as do many triggerfishes and groupers. In nature they often behave aggressively toward others of their species. In aquariums, such aggression can be relentless, culminating in the injury or death of the recipient. Angelfishes and butterflyfishes some-

Figure 79 *The blackedge moray* (Gymnothorax nigromarginatus) *is solitary, living in crevices in the reef. Photographed at Bonaire, Netherlands Antilles, 85 feet.*

Figure 80 *The banded butterflyfish* (Chaetodon striatus) *is usually seen in pairs or small groups of three to five individuals. Photographed at Bonaire, Netherlands Antilles, 75 feet.*

Figure 81 *The creole wrasse* (Clepticus parrai) *and other schooling fishes are inherently social (also see Color Plate 11c). These creole wrasses are feeding on plankton over a deep reef. Photographed from below at Bonaire, Netherlands Antilles, 70 feet.*

times travel in pairs (Figure 80) or small groups. Such associations are often permanent, but not always. Other species are solitary. In aquariums, aggression can be reduced by keeping only one specimen of a solitary species.

SCHOOLING FISHES

Fishes that form schools are inherently social (Figure 81). Adjustment to aquarium conditions seems to be faster if at least two are kept together. When decorating the aquarium, (see Chapter 9), leave enough open space at one end or near the center for fishes to school.

CRYPTIC FISHES

Some cryptic fishes hide; others rest motionless on the substratum or against objects, moving only occasionally. Depending on the species, a cryptic fish can possess cryptic coloration, fleshy appendages that enable them to blend with the surroundings, or both. The fleshy appendages of some scorpionfishes

Figure 82 *Fleshy appendages of the barbfish* (Scorpaena brasiliensis), *a scorpionfish, render it nearly invisible against a background of coral rubble and algae (also see Color Plate 9b). Photographed at Key Largo, Florida, 27 feet.*

Figure 83 *The peacock flounder* (Bothus lunatus) *is nearly invisible when partly buried in sand. In captivity, tropical flounders should be provided with a loose substratum such as coral hash. Photographed at Bonaire, Netherlands Antilles, 9 feet.*

give them the appearance of rocks covered with algae and detritus (Figure 82). Other fish species such as flounders are adept at rapid changes in coloration and pattern, enabling them to blend into the background. Flounders assume the coloration of the substratum and further disguise their presence by remaining motionless (Figure 83). In captivity they require a loose substratum, preferably coral hash (see Table 2 and Figure 24b).

Nocturnal species such as cardinalfishes, morays, and squirrelfishes are cryptic during daylight hours, although they can be trained to emerge and feed during the day. They require adequate shelter, preferably locations that are dark when the room is bright.

Figure 84 *Sea anemone* (Condylactis gigantea; *also see Color Plate 13a). Photographed at Bonaire, Netherlands Antilles, 45 feet.*

Figure 85 *The long-spined sea urchin* (Diadema antillarum) *wedges itself into a crevice during the day, but emerges at night to feed on algae. Photographed at Pine Cay, Turks and Caicos Islands, British West Indies, 22 feet (night).*

Figure 86 *The banded coral shrimp* (Stenopus hispidus) *is a popular aquarium animal. In nature, banded coral shrimps are often found in pairs. Photographed at Bonaire, Netherlands Antilles, 25 feet (night).*

Figure 87 *The crab* Dromidia *protects itself by attaching bits of live (and largely inedible) sponge to its back. The sponge grows and forms a protective shield over the crab. The crab shown is feeding on polyps of orange tube corals* (Tubastrea aurea). *Photographed at Bonaire, Netherlands Antilles, 28 feet (night).*

INVERTEBRATES

Many species of sea anemones are solitary (Figure 84); others clump together. Sea anemones kept in marine aquariums often change locations, moving slowly from one place to another. Some species prefer sites with good water movement. If circulation is inadequate, they commonly become established near the airlift outlets.

Some sea urchins retire to individual shelter spaces during the day and emerge at night to feed on algae (Figure 85). In dirty aquariums they congregate on the inside glass surfaces and décor to scavenge algae. This activity can scratch the glass and causes extensive damage to plastic decorations.

Most shrimps (Figure 86) and crabs (Figure 87) maintained in marine aquariums do not warrant special consideration in terms of social requirements. All, however, should be provided with adequate shelter spaces.

CHAPTER

14 Supplemental Light

Synopsis *Except for some species of sea anemones, animals kept in conventional marine aquariums do not require supplemental light. Its presence encourages the growth of spontaneous or nuisance algae, and this is undesirable. Ornamental algae, which are larger and more attractive than spontaneous species, can be purchased from dealers and cultivated intentionally. Conditions that are conducive to growing ornamental algae also enhance the growth of spontaneous forms. If you keep ornamental species, allot extra maintenance time to control spontaneous algal growths. Keep ornamental algae in your aquarium for esthetic reasons only; any additional benefits are dubious. Although all algae take up nitrogen, water quality is not improved because dissolved organic carbon is liberated in the process. Nor do any of the algae help maintain stable pH values above 8.0, serve as an important food supplement for aquarium animals, or create the appearance of a coral reef, as some people believe. Shallow aquariums are preferable to deep ones for growing ornamental algae. Grow-Lux® lamps are undesirable. Use cool white or daylight fluorescent lamps, or mix them. Buy the highest wattage lamps that will fit into the overhead reflector. Replace fluorescent lamps every 6 months. Purchase a rapid-start lamp fixture that can be plugged into an electric timer. Operate it on a cycle of 8 hours on and 16 hours off.*

Freshwater aquarists can select from an impressive array of decorative flowering plants, but marine aquarists are mostly restricted to a few species of algae. Supplemental light from lamps placed directly over an aquarium promotes algal growths impossible to match if the only illumination is from room lamps or a distant window. *Seaweeds,* or *macroalgae,* the plants grown most commonly in marine aquariums, are large and visible; the remaining algal species are the *phytoplankton*, or *microalgae*, which are microscopic. Microalgae are not grown intentionally in aquariums. *With the exception of some species of sea anemones, animals kept in conventional marine aquariums do not require supplemental light. Its presence encourages the growth of spontaneous or nuisance algae, and this is undesirable.*

SPONTANEOUS AND ORNAMENTAL ALGAE

From an aquarist's standpoint, algae can be placed into one of three categories: (*1*) uninvited seaweeds that appear spontaneously and grow attached to stationary objects; (*2*) uninvited microalgae suspended in the water and attached to stationary objects, sometimes forming dense mats in neglected aquariums; and (*3*) ornamental algae such as *Acetabularia*, *Caulerpa*, and other green seaweeds purchased from a dealer for intentional cultivation and present by invitation (Figure 88).

Algae that appear on the decorations, gravel, and inside glass surfaces of marine aquariums are included in the first two categories. I shall refer to these collectively as *spontaneous algae* because they appear eventually whether or not you want them. Their presence is mostly a nuisance, but they are difficult to discourage if supplemental light has been added to enhance the growth of ornamental species. *Conditions that are conducive to growing ornamental algae also enhance the growth of spontaneous forms*. The result is more time spent keeping the aquarium clean, which often includes preventing spontaneous algae from overgrowing and smothering ornamental species.

PRESUMED BENEFITS OF ALGAE

Many aquarists believe that algae (*1*) improve water quality by taking up nitrogen, (*2*) assist in maintaining the pH above 8.0, (*3*) provide an important food source for aquarium animals, and (*4*) promote a "natural" appearance similar to a coral reef. The evidence, however, does not support these claims. Bombarding conventional marine aquariums with supplemental light for purposes of growing either spontaneous or ornamental algae accomplishes little that is positive (see Chapter 15, Myth 7).

Nitrate is the only form of nitrogen that increases in marine aquariums, and the concentration is controlled easily and efficiently by regular partial water changes. Growing spontaneous

Figure 88 Caulerpa sertulariodes *is a green seaweed commonly cultivated in marine aquariums (also see Color Plate 16a). Photographed in Florida Bay, Key Largo, Florida, 3 feet.*

or ornamental algae to lower the nitrate concentration is accomplished at the expense of adding dissolved organic carbon, a trade-off that by no means is beneficial. Healthy algae are "leaky," exuding organic compounds into the water continuously. Algae that are damaged by animals feeding on them or during routine maintenance leak organic substances even more rapidly. As explained in Chapter 5, some organic compounds released by algae either are pigmented or react with other substances in the water to produce unsightly greenish-yellow pigments. An increase in the dissolved organic carbon concentration (both colorless and pigmented compounds) provides added nutrients for heterotrophic bacteria, and the overall effect is to raise the metabolic level of the aquarium. Other algal products are known toxins of marine animals.

Photosynthesis, the biochemical process that plants use to synthesize tissues by using light energy, is chemically reductive: Carbon dioxide is taken up and oxygen is liberated, which raises the pH of the water. Respiration, however, is chemically oxidative: Oxygen is consumed and carbon dioxide is released, which lowers the pH. Photosynthesis occurs only in light, but respiration takes place continuously in both light and darkness. Under supplemental light, photosynthesis overrides respiration, presenting a momentary illusion that the overall effect on pH is to raise it. *Lush algal growths actually destabilize the pH by causing it to fluctuate.* Periodic addition of baking soda combined with continuous, heavy aeration by airlift pumping to drive off excess carbon dioxide is the most effective means of pH control (see Chapters 6 and 10).

As explained in Chapter 11, animals kept in marine aquariums do not need to ingest plant matter. The use of spontaneous algae as a dietary supplement is seldom harmful, although neither is it measurably beneficial. Many ornamental algae (for example, *Caulerpa*) produce and retain toxic compounds in their tissues, which renders them unpalatable to marine animals. These species are unlikely to be eaten, and the food value they offer ranges from minimal to none.

Marine aquariums look unnatural and unkempt when dominated by spontaneous algae. The appearance is reminiscent of tepid lagoons, turtle grass beds, mangrove islands, and other shallow areas of the tropics and subtropics, but not coral reefs (Figure 89). Other algal groups (for example, the *turf algae*) predominate on coral reefs, where their growth is checked by continuous grazing activities of herbivorous fishes and invertebrates. Ornamental algae available from dealers are not included among the turf algae, and few are representative of the dominant algae found on coral reefs.

To summarize, spontaneous algae offer no demonstrated benefit. Their growth should be discouraged. If you decide to grow ornamental algae, do so for the only reason that makes sense—because they make attractive additions—and allot the necessary time for extra maintenance to control spontaneous algal growths.

SUPPLEMENTAL LIGHT REQUIREMENTS

Most of the tropical and subtropical seaweeds maintained as ornamental algae in marine aquariums require lots of light. Because water absorbs light, the distance the light must travel affects how well ornamental algae survive and grow. *Shallow aquariums (low models, see Chapter 1) are preferable to deep ones for growing ornamental algae.* Grow-Lux® lamps (fluorescent lamps sold widely to aquarists) have two undesirable features. First,

Figure 89 *Many aquarists mistakenly believe that lush growths of nuisance algae render a visual effect similar to that of a coral reef. This underwater photograph depicts a tepid, subtropical lagoon in midsummer (also see Color Plate 16c). The scene resembles a carelessly maintained marine aquarium overgrown with nuisance algae, not a coral reef. Photographed in Florida Bay, Key Marathon, Florida, 5 feet.*

the light output is of lower intensity than cool white and daylight fluorescent lamps. Second, the coloration imparted to animals and other objects is pinkish and unnatural. *Use cool white or daylight fluorescent lamps, or mix them. Buy the highest wattage lamps that will fit into the overhead reflector*. Many hardware stores have large selections. The intensity of fluorescent lamps declines steadily and almost imperceptibly with time, so lamps should be replaced every 6 months. Purchase a rapid-start lamp fixture that can be plugged into an electric timer. Operate it on a cycle of 8 hours on and 16 hours off.

CHAPTER

15 Aquarium Mythology

Synopsis *Aquarium myths are practices based on pseudoscience and anecdotal evidence. They should be abandoned in favor of empiricism, which is based on observation.* Myth 1—Water treatment devices eliminate the need for partial water changes. *Aquarium water deteriorates with time, and regular partial water changes are desirable.* Myth 2—Plastic filtrants are comparable or even superior to gravel in terms of biological performance. *Plastic filtrants are substantially inferior to similar volumes of gravel.* Myth 3—Long-lasting activated carbon is superior in removing dissolved organic carbon. *Some kinds of activated carbon last longer than others, but this is attributable to their limited capacity to take up a broad size range of organic molecules. In this sense they are inferior.* Myth 4—Resin beads are superior for removing unwanted substances from marine aquarium waters. *Ion exchange resins are ineffective in saline waters. Other types of resins manufactured for the removal of dissolved organic carbon are inferior to activated carbon.* Myth 5—Nitrite is very toxic. *Nitrite is toxic in freshwaters but appears to be largely nontoxic in saline waters. Nitrite in a marine aquarium is nothing to worry about.* Myth 6—Nitrate is very toxic. *Nitrate is essentially nontoxic, even at very high concentrations.* Myth 7—The overall effect of algae is beneficial. *Algae contribute little that is beneficial; in some instances their presence can be detrimental.* Myth 8—Marine fishes are stressed less at low specific gravity values. *Nothing in the extensive literature on fish physiology suggests that lowering the specific gravity of a marine aquarium renders the environment less stressful.* Myth 9—Proper temperature acclimation includes floating newly acquired marine animals in their plastic bags. *Temperature acclimation involves physiological* *changes that take days or weeks, not minutes or hours. Floating achieves nothing. Release newly acquired animals into a quarantine aquarium as soon as you get home.*

By one definition, *myths* are traditional stories that serve to explain practices, beliefs, or natural phenomena; by another they are unfounded or false notions. Both definitions apply to the marine aquarium hobby in which traditional stories, having evolved into practices and beliefs about how nature functions, are reinforced by unfounded notions disguised as expert advice. No trap set for the unwitting aquarist is camouflaged more cleverly, simply because statements purportedly based on experimental evidence are difficult to confirm or disprove.

At the center is the expert, often a marine aquarist who has written an article or book. But the advice offered is seldom predicated on direct *empirical* evidence; that is, evidence obtained through observation using accepted experimental methods. Typically, statements intended to explain aquarium practices and beliefs are mosaics of experimental results obtained second-hand from literature pertaining to wastewater treatment, coral reef ecology, and other disciplines related only remotely to marine aquarium keeping. When taken out of context and misinterpreted, such "evidence" is actually a compendium of unfounded and false notions, not the result of legitimate science. Seldom, if ever, can results obtained in other fields of science and technology be applied unilaterally to marine aquariums.

In this final chapter I draw attention to the difference between empiricism and charlatanism. In doing so I hope to establish a rift between experimental evidence, with its vibrant pulse, and anecdotal evidence, which leaves the mirror of truth unfogged. Many authors of marine aquarium literature come dangerously close to violating Mark Twain's third rule of writing: "That the personages in a tale shall be alive, except in the case of the corpses, and that always the reader shall be able to tell the corpses from the others."

MYTH 1—WATER TREATMENT DEVICES ELIMINATE THE NEED FOR PARTIAL WATER CHANGES

The most presumptuous myth of all is embodied in the belief that the chemistry of marine aquarium waters can be kept in a semblance of steady state by power filters, foam fractionators, ozonators, and other water treatment devices. Almost nothing is

known about chemical change
By logical extension even less
measures. Only chemical facto
easily—inorganic nitrogen, alkal
gravity—ordinarily are monitored by aq
tentious marine aquarium contains thous
pounds. We know nothing about the rates a
disappear, recombine in altered states, or acc
we even guess which of them might be benefi
either actually or potentially.

It cannot be stated at this time whether a foam fra
ozonator is beneficial because "beneficial" has not been
from the standpoint of legitimate hypothesis testing, a cr
of the scientific method. Once formulated and stated in the
propriate terms, a hypothesis is subjected to rigorous compa
son: in this example, against an *experimental control* consisting of
an identical group of animals or plants treated in the same way except for the absence of foam fractionation or ozonation. Appropriate hypotheses describing the presumed benefits of these and other processes have yet to be formulated. That being the case, any supposed "benefits" must be considered speculative and therefore unconfirmed. Not surprisingly, the utility of both foam fractionation and ozonation remains a mystery to everyone, including manufacturers who falsely claim knowledge that somehow has eluded the entire scientific community. The same can be said for power filters and other devices without demonstrated utility.

MYTH 2—PLASTIC FILTRANTS ARE SUPERIOR TO GRAVEL IN TERMS OF BIOLOGICAL PERFORMANCE

From the standpoint of biological filtration, plastic filtrants are substantially inferior to similar volumes of gravel. Advertisers who claim the reverse invariably refer to the large surface areas of their products. However, surface area is only one factor by which performance of packed filters is rated. Among the host of other factors is *void fraction* (also called *porosity*), which is the fraction of a packed filter that is empty space. Filter bacteria attach to solid surfaces, not empty space. The larger the void fraction the poorer the biological performance. In contrast, gravel grains are solid, not hollow, so void fraction is accounted for almost entirely by the spaces among grains.

ltrants are manufactured in a variety of shapes (for
llow spheres and cylinders). Many designs incorpo-
spikes, and similar projections in an effort to in-
e area. Nonetheless, the void fraction of all such
ically exceeds 0.9. In other words, 90% or more of a
containing plastic filtrants is empty space. Reduc-
f the filtrant material while retaining the same de-
the surface area of a given filtrant volume, but
tays the same.

erms, a container of plastic filtrant must be many
n one of gravel before comparable performance
y Adams of Three Rivers Community College
necticut) and I devised a mathematical model
erformance of 1/4-inch gravel and a 1-inch plastic
nufacturer's rated void fraction.[20] Both filters
assumed to be conditioned. We based performance on capacity to remove 50% of the ammonia from a stream of water in a single pass. The equations revealed huge disparities. The depth of the gravel necessary to achieve 50% ammonia removal was approximately 8 1/2 inches; that of the plastic filtrant was 42 feet.

MYTH 3—LONG-LASTING ACTIVATED CARBON IS SUPERIOR IN REMOVING DISSOLVED ORGANIC CARBON

Activated carbon is manufactured from many different materials, often for specific applications. Activated carbons can have pores that are predominantly large, small, intermediate, or a mix of several sizes. Those with uniformly small pore sizes are superior for air filtration, although sometimes they perform poorly in aquatic applications. Materials having small pore sizes give the appearance of lasting a long time, but this is because they are incapable of taking up large molecules. Pigmented portions of the dissolved organic carbon in aquarium waters are composed partly of humic and fulvic acids, many of large molecular size. The most effective kinds of activated carbon in water treatment applications have a mix of pore sizes ranging from small to large. At saturation, additional molecules cannot be taken up regardless of pore size. If the material is not replaced, desaturation be-

[20]See Spotte (1992) in Additional Reading ("Advanced Aquarists" section).

gins to occur. During *desaturation* the molecules taken up start to leach back into the water.

MYTH 4—RESIN BEADS ARE SUPERIOR FOR REMOVING UNWANTED SUBSTANCES FROM MARINE AQUARIUM WATERS

Plastic resins in the form of tiny beads are used for many applications in water treatment. The surfaces of *ion exchange resins* are impregnated with ions of positive or negative electrical charges, and sometimes a combination. Specific ions in the water are exchanged with harmless ions of similar charge from the resin surfaces. For example, ammonium ions (NH_4^+) in water might be exchanged for sodium ions (Na^+) at the resin surfaces. Freshwaters treated with such a resin gain a little sodium, which is harmless, but relinquish toxic ammonia. Ion exchange resins perform effectively in freshwaters and are used widely in water-softening applications. However, saline waters have high concentrations of ions that compete with the ions intended for removal. This causes the resin surfaces to become saturated rapidly, at which point ion exchange ceases. In seawater and artificial seawaters, activity is probably limited to a few minutes, after which the resins are saturated and cease to function.

Polymeric resins are manufactured to remove dissolved organic carbon from water. Two such resins tested in our laboratory several years ago removed only 17% and 15% of the total organic carbon from marine aquarium waters after, respectively, 96 and 92 hours of application. Neither performed as capably as the least effective of four types of activated carbon tested in later experiments.

MYTH 5—NITRITE IS VERY TOXIC

Nitrite is an important toxicant in freshwater fish culture, causing *brown-blood disease*, or *methemoglobinemia*. Nitrite is assimilated from water into the blood via the gills, where it reacts with the iron in hemoglobin to produce *methemoglobin*. *Hemoglobin* is the blood respiratory pigment that takes up oxygen and distributes it to the tissues. Methemoglobin is substantially inferior to hemoglobin in terms of its capacity to bind and release oxygen. The result of methemoglobinemia is respiratory distress, culminating in death.

The toxic threshold of nitrite for marine fishes is much higher than it is for freshwater fishes because chloride and calcium are comparatively more concentrated in seawater and artificial seawaters. Chloride and calcium exert powerful protective effects. Calcium's protective mechanism is less well understood and evidently is species dependent to some extent. Chloride and nitrite ions compete for sites on the gill surface. These sites are entry points into the blood. Chloride is a major constituent of seawater and artificial seawaters, present at concentrations of approximately 19,000 mg/L. In contrast, the nitrite ion (NO_3^-) concentration of aquarium water seldom exceeds 10 mg/L (approximately 3 mg/L of nitrite-N; see Chapter 6). In such circumstances, the chances are exceedingly high that chloride will arrive at gill sites of captive marine fishes first and occupy them to the exclusion of nitrite.

In the species of marine fishes tested to date, nitrite-N concentrations of 100 mg/L and even greater have, on occasion, induced limited adverse effects. Typically, however, no effects have been observed at these unusually high concentrations. Some of the experiments have included larvae, which are often more sensitive than adults to waterborne toxicants. To my knowledge, nitrite toxicity has never been demonstrated to be a limiting factor in marine aquarium keeping.

MYTH 6—NITRATE IS VERY TOXIC

Nitrate is even less toxic than nitrite. Marine aquaculturists have recorded concentrations exceeding 1000 mg/L of nitrate-N (approximately 4400 mg/L of NO_3^-) without any observable effect on cultured food fishes. In the absence of contrary evidence, 50 mg/L of nitrate-N (220 mg/L of NO_3^-) can be considered a safe upper limit for marine aquarium fishes.

MYTH 7—THE OVERALL EFFECT OF ALGAE IS BENEFICIAL

Marine algae remove ammonia, nitrite, nitrate, and phosphate from water for use in their own tissues during growth. Awareness of these processes has encouraged the belief that seaweeds induce a marked positive effect on the quality of water in marine aquariums. However, ammonia and nitrite are consistently low in aquariums with conditioned subgravel filters, and the concentration of nitrate, which increases gradually, can be reduced by regular partial water changes. More stringent measures of nitrate control might be necessary if nitrate proved to be even mildly toxic, but this is not the case. Phosphate is not toxic either and appears to reach steady state in conditioned aquariums. Additional efforts directed toward removing any of these compounds are therefore of doubtful value.

Encouraging lush growths of spontaneous algae (see Chapter 14) appears superficially to be a harmless activity, were it not for what algae *add* to the environment. Marine biologists have long recognized that seaweeds are "leaky," losing to the environment much of the organic carbon fixed during photosynthesis. Intense photosynthesis by a large crop of seaweeds adds considerably to the concentration of dissolved organic carbon in aquarium water. As described in Chapter 14, an increase in dissolved organic carbon has two negative effects. First, some of this material either is pigmented or reacts with substances already present to produce unsightly greenish-yellow compounds. Second, high concentrations of dissolved organic carbon, whether pigmented or colorless, encourage large populations of heterotrophic bacteria. The result is accelerated *eutrophication*, a condition characteristic of polluted natural waters. *Eutrophic* environments contain high concentrations of nutrients—mainly nitrogen, carbon, and phosphorus—that enhance bacterial and plant growth. Aquarium waters containing abnormally high nutrient concentrations are also eutrophic. Removing nitrogen while adding carbon does little to reverse the situation, especially when potentially adverse effects of carbon compounds in aquarium waters are less well understood.

MYTH 8—MARINE FISHES ARE STRESSED LESS AT LOW SPECIFIC GRAVITY VALUES

Freshwater and marine fishes regulate the water and ion balance of their blood and tissues independently of the external environment. Depending on the substance being moved and its concentration, the transport mechanism involved can be *passive* (also called *diffusional*) or *active*. During active transport, ions are pumped across membranes, often against a greater concentration of the same ions on the other side. Active transport is *work* in a physiological sense, so energy is required. Passive transport requires no energy.

Although freshwaters are considerably more dilute than the oceans, both freshwater and marine fishes have blood and tissue ion concentrations that are approximately one-third the strength of seawater. The passive and active transport processes of freshwater fishes prevent the blood and tissues from becoming depleted of sodium, potassium, chloride, and other essential ions. Ordinarily, freshwater fishes drink very little water, although water enters anyway through the permeable gills and skin. Water in excess of the amount needed for metabolic functions is discharged into the environment. However, ions are conserved, resulting in blood and tissues that are "saltier" than the outside environment.

Marine fishes are faced with the opposite problem: the prospect of too little blood and tissue water and the accumulation of excess ions. To conserve water (that is, water devoid of ions), marine fishes drink seawater continuously, retaining the water component and excreting excess ions mainly through the gills. By "excess ions" I mean those in excess of amounts required to maintain blood and tissue ion concentrations at one-third seawater strength.

In neither situation—freshwater or seawater—is the regulation of tissue water and ions demonstrably stressful in any conventional sense, unless stress is defined strictly in terms of energy expenditure. The conjecture that normal physiological processes are somehow rendered less stressful to marine fishes by lowering the specific gravity is therefore surprising.

As just explained, the blood and tissues of marine fishes contain ions at lower concentrations than the surrounding seawater. However, the outward movement of ions (that is, from fish to seawater) involves more than differences in concentration. Membranes of living tissues are selective in terms of the ions that pass across them. Selectivity is achieved in part by differences in electrical charges on either side of a membrane. This disparity allows certain ions to move passively outward from the fish and into the environment at extremely low energy expenditures by alleviating the need to "pump" them across actively. Some marine fishes appear to rely on such charge differences to control ion flow; in others, the excretion of major ions appears to be truly passive, requiring no energy expenditure. It is doubtful whether lowering the specific gravity of an aquarium affects any potential difference in ion concentration between the external (seawater) and internal (physiological) environments. Consequently, the exercise seems pointless.

MYTH 9—PROPER TEMPERATURE ACCLIMATION INVOLVES FLOATING NEWLY ACQUIRED MARINE ANIMALS IN THEIR PLASTIC BAGS

Aquarists still believe that proper acclimation of newly acquired animals includes flotation. During *flotation,* a fish or invertebrate imprisoned inside its plastic transport bag is floated briefly in the aquarium before being released. According to adherents of this practice, flotation allows the bag's occupant time to adjust its body temperature to that of the aquarium.

Marine aquarium fishes and invertebrates are *ectothermic* (cold blooded). Their body temperatures and the temperature of the external environment are similar. However, *temperature acclimation* involves physiological changes that take days or weeks, not minutes or hours. The water temperature inside a plastic bag equilibrates rapidly with that of the aquarium. However, the animal inside the bag has not adjusted at all. Flotation achieves nothing. Keeping marine animals confined in plastic bags filled with dirty water is more harmful than simply releasing them into a quarantine aquarium as soon as you get home.

Additional Reading

The books and articles listed represent a cross section of literature of interest to marine aquarists. Marine aquarium keeping requires thought and study, and accomplished aquarists read and collect information on the subject. Many of the books are out of print, although they sometimes appear in used bookstores. Articles from serial publications can be photocopied at public libraries, requested on interlibrary loan, or obtained from the publishers. The university publications listed can be obtained through Sea Grant offices (if in print) or interlibrary loan.

Beginning and Intermediate Aquarists

Anonymous. Undated. *Establishing an Exciting Marine Aquarium Simple as A-B-C*. Aquarium Systems, Eastlake (Ohio), 8 pp.

Anonymous. 1968. *Some Guides to Designing, Building and Operating Salt Water Aquarium Systems*. Triton Aquatics, Levittown (Pennsylvania), 36 pp.

Anonymous. 1981. *Starting and Maintaining a Marine Aquarium*. Publication No. 1287, Cooperative Extension Service, Mississippi State University, Mississippi State (Mississippi), 23 pp.

Axelrod, H. R. and W. Vorderwinkler. 1956. *Salt-water Aquarium Fish*. Sterling Publishing Co., New York, 160 pp.

Axelrod, H. R. and W. Vorderwinkler. 1965. *Salt-water Aquarium Fish*, Revised edition. T.F.H. Publications, Jersey City (New Jersey), 352 pp.

Baensch, H. A. 1983. *Marine Aquarist's Manual*. Tetra-Press, Melle, Germany, 98 pp. [Published originally in 1976 as *Klein Seewasser Praxis*, TetraWerke, Melle, West Germany.]

Blasiola, G. C. II. 1991. *The New Saltwater Aquarium Handbook*. Barron's Educational Series, Hauppauge (New York), 134 pp.

Bower, C. E. 1975. *Keeping a Marine Aquarium: A Guide for Teachers*. Children's Museum of Hartford, Hartford (Connecticut), 24 pp.

Bower, C. E. 1980. Saltwater aquariums: water quality without water analysis. *Freshwater and Marine Aquarium* 3(4): 44–46, 59.

Bower, C. E. 1983. *The Basic Marine Aquarium: A Simplified, Modern Approach to the Care of Saltwater Fishes*. Charles C Thomas, Springfield (Illinois), xx + 269 pp.

Braker, W. P. 1966. *Enjoy a Saltwater Aquarium*. Pet Library, New York, 32 pp.

Chave, E. H. and P. S. Lobel. 1974. *Marine and Freshwater Aquarium Systems for Tropical Animals*. UNIHI-SEAGRANT-AR-74-01, University of Hawaii, Honolulu, vii + 88 pp.

Cox, G. F. 1972. *Tropical Marine Aquaria*. Grosset & Dunlap, New York, 159 pp.

Cust, G. and G. Cox. 1972. *Tropical Aquarium Fishes: Freshwater and Marine.* Hamlyn, New York, 144 pp.

Dal Vesco, V., W. Klausewitz, B. Peyronel, and E. Tortonese. 1974. *Aquarium Life.* Chartwell Books, Secaucus (New Jersey), 248 pp. [Published originally in 1974 (title unstated) by Arnoldo Mondadori Editore, Milan.]

Dewey, D. 1979. Brine shrimp. Part two. *Freshwater and Marine Aquaium* 2(5): 58–63, 66.

Dutta, R. 1972. *Beginner's Guide to Tropical Fish: Fish Tanks, Coldwater Aquarium Fish, Pond Fish and Marines.* Pelham Books, London, 184 pp.

Garibaldi, L. 1969. *Cool Marines.* Special Publication No. 2, San Francisco Aquarium Society, San Francisco, 12 pp.

King, J. M. and W. E. Kelley. 1976. *Marine Aquariums: Principle and Practice.* Aquarium Systems, Eastlake (Ohio), 26 pp.

Kingsford, E. 1975. *Treatment of Exotic Marine Fish Diseases.* Palmetto Publishing Co., St. Petersburg (Florida), 90 pp. + index.

Lee, R. S. 1976. *Construction and Maintenance of Classroom Aquaria.* Marine Science Curriculum Aid No. 2, Alaska Sea Grant Program, University of Alaska, Anchorage, 17 pp.

Miklosz, J. C. 1978a. Basic seawater chemistry. Part one. *Pet Age* 8(4): 22, 24, 25.

Miklosz, J. C. 1978b. Basic seawater chemistry. Part two. *Pet Age* 8(6): 38, 39, 41, 42.

Miklosz, J. C. 1979a. Basic seawater chemistry. Part three. *Pet Age* 8(8): 44, 45, 48.

Miklosz, J. C. 1979b. Basic seawater chemistry. Part four. *Pet Age* 8(10): 12–19.

Moe, M. A. Jr. 1992. *The Marine Aquarium Handbook: Beginner to Breeder,* New edition. Green Turtle Publications, Plantation (Florida), 318 pp.

Mowka, E. J. Jr. 1979. *The Instant Ocean® Handbook.* Aquarium Systems, Mentor (Ohio), 20 pp.

Mowka, E. J. Jr. 1981. *The Seawater Manual: Fundamentals of Water Chemistry for Marine Aquarists.* Aquarium Systems, Mentor (Ohio), 43 pp.

Palko, B. J. Undated (circa 1982). *A Balanced Marine Aquarium.* PB82-12871, National Technical Information Service, Springfield (Virginia), 24 pp.

Simkatis, H. 1958. *Salt-water Fishes for the Home Aquarium.* J. P. Lippincott, Philadelphia, 254 pp.

Spotte, S. 1973. *Marine Aquarium Keeping: The Science, Animals, and Art.* John Wiley & Sons, New York, xv + 171 pp.

Stoskopf, M. A. and S. Citino. *AAZV Workshop on Tropical Marine Fish Medicine.* Waikiki Aquarium, Honolulu, 169 pp.

Straughan, R. P. L. 1969. *The Salt-water Aquarium in the Home,* Second edition. A. S. Barnes, New Brunswick (New Jersey), 360 pp.

Tullock, J. H. 1982. Light in the marine aquarium. *Freshwater and Marine Aquarium* 5(4): 7–9.

Valenti, R. J. 1968. *The Salt Water Aquarium Manual.* Aquarium Stock Co., New York, ix + 162 pp.

Wallace, N. L. 1985. The classroom saltwater aquarium. *Carolina Tips* (Carolina Biological Supply Company) 48(8): 29–32.

Wickler, W. 1973. *The Marine Aquarium.* T.F.H. Publications, Neptune City (New Jersey), 112 pp. [Published originally in 1963 as *Das Meeresaquarium,* Frank'sche Verlagshandlung, W. Keller and Co., Stuttgart.]

Wilkie, D. W. 1971. *Some Hints for Maintaining Marine Animals in the Home or Classroom,* Second edition. Scripps Aquarium Publication No. 3, Scripps Institution of Oceanography, La Jolla (California), 22 pp.

Advanced Aquarists

Adams, S. M. (editor). 1990. *Biological Indicators of Stress in Fish.* Symposium 8, American Fisheries Society, Bethesda (Maryland), v + 191 pp.

Adey, W. H. and K. Loveland. 1991. *Dynamic Aquaria: Building Living Ecosystems.* Academic Press, San Diego, xv + 643 pp.

Anonymous. 1991. *Engineering of Intensive Aquaculture: Proceedings from the Aquaculture Symposium, Cornell University, April 4–6, 1991.* NRAES-49, Northeast Regional Agricultural Service, Ithaca (New York), v + 348 pp.

Bidwell, J. P. and S. Spotte. 1985. *Artificial Seawaters: Formulas and Methods.* Jones & Bartlett, Boston, 349 pp.

Colt, J. 1984. *Computation of Dissolved Gas Concentrations in Water as Functions of Temperature,*

Salinity, and Pressure. Special Publication No. 14, American Fisheries Society, Bethesda (Maryland), vi + 154 pp.

Committee on Marine Invertebrates. 1981. *Laboratory Animal Management: Marine Invertebrates*. National Academy Press, Washington (D.C.), x + 382 pp.

Ferguson, H. W. (editor). 1989. *Systemic Pathology of Fish: A Text and Atlas of Comparative Tissue Responses in Diseases of Teleosts*. Iowa State University Press, Ames, ix + 263 pp.

Graaf, F. de. 1973. *Marine Aquarium Guide*. Pet Library, Harrison (New Jersey), 284 pp. [Reprinted by T.F.H. Publications; published originally in 1968 as *Handboek voor het Tropisch Zeewater Aquarium*, A.J.G. Strengholt N.V., Amsterdam.]

Klontz, G. W. 1973. *Syllabus of Fish Health Management*. TAMU-SG-74-401, Texas A & M University, College Station, x + 165 pp.

Manning, M. J. and M. F. Tatner (editors). 1985. *Fish Immunology*. Academic Press, London, xi + 374 pp.

McDaniel, D. (editor). 1979. *Procedures for the Detection and Identification of Certain Fish Pathogens*, Revised edition. American Fisheries Society, Bethesda (Maryland), ix + 118 pp.

Mercer, J. T. (editor). 1974. *Conference for the Tropical Fish Institute of America, July 11–12, 1974*. College of Veterinary Medicine and Georgia Center for Continuing Education, Athens (Georgia), unpaginated.

Moe, M. A. Jr. 1989. *The Marine Aquarium Reference: Systems and Invertebrates*. Green Turtle Publications, Plantation (Florida), 510 pp.

Overstreet, R. M. 1978. *Marine Maladies? Worms, Germs, and Other Symbionts from the Northern Gulf of Mexico*. MASGP-78-021, Gulf Coast Research Laboratory, Ocean Springs (Mississippi), 140 pp.

Sindermann, C. J. 1990. *Principal Diseases of Marine Fish and Shellfish*, Volume 1, Second edition. Academic Press, San Diego, x + 521 pp.

Spotte, S. 1979a. *Fish and Invertebrate Culture: Water Management in Closed Systems*, Second edition. John Wiley & Sons, New York, xvi + 179 pp.

Spotte, S. 1979b. *Seawater Aquariums: The Captive Environment*. John Wiley & Sons, New York, xi + 413 pp.

Spotte, S. 1992. *Captive Seawater Fishes: Science and Technology*. John Wiley & Sons, New York, xxii + 942 pp.

Stoskopf, M.K. (editor). 1993. *Fish Medicine*. W.B. Saunders Co., Philadelphia, xix + 882 pp.

Stumm, W. and J. J. Morgan. 1981. *Aquatic Chemistry: An Introduction Emphasizing Chemical Equilibria in Natural Waters*, Second edition. John Wiley & Sons, New York, xiv + 780 pp.

Identification Guides

Identification guides provide the names of marine animals frequently kept in aquariums. Many species do not have common names and are referred to only by their scientific names. Identification guides supply other useful information, such as length at maturity, social behavior, food preferences, and habitat characteristics.

Allen, G. R. 1979. *Butterfly and Angelfishes of the World*, Volume 2. John Wiley & Sons, New York, pp. 149-352. [also see Steene 1977.]

Allen, G. R. 1980. *The Anemonefishes of the World: Species, Care and Breeding*, English edition. Aquarium Systems, Mentor (Ohio), 104 pp.

Böhlke, J. E. and C. C. G. Chaplin. 1968. *Fishes of the Bahamas and Adjacent Tropical Waters*. Academy of Natural Sciences of Philadelphia, Philadelphia, xxiii + 771 pp.

Burgess, W. E., H. R. Axelrod, and R. E. Hunziker III. 1988. *Dr. Burgess's Atlas of Marine Aquarium Fishes*. T.F.H. Publications, Neptune City (New Jersey), 768 pp.

Carcasson, R. H. 1977. *A Field Guide to the Coral Reef Fishes of the Indian and West Pacific Oceans*. William Collins Sons, London, 320 pp.

Colin, P. I. 1978. *Marine Invertebrates and Plants of the Living Reef*. T.F.H. Publications, Neptune City (New Jersey), 512 pp.

Hoese, H. D. and R. H. Moore. 1977. *Fishes of the Gulf of Mexico: Texas, Louisiana, and Adjacent Waters*. Texas A & M University, College Station, xv + 327 pp.

Humann, P. 1989. *Reef Fish Identification: Florida, Caribbean, Bahamas*. Vaughn Press, Orlando (Florida), 267 pp. + index.

Humann, P. 1992. *Reef Creature Identification: Florida,*

Caribbean, Bahamas. Vaughn Press, Orlando (Florida), 320 pp. + index.

Littler, D. S., M. M. Littler, K. E. Bucher, and J. N. Norris. 1989. *Marine Plants of the Caribbean: A Field Guide from Florida to Brazil*. Smithsonian Institution Press, Washington (D.C.), 263 pp.

Marshall, T. C. 1964. *Fishes of the Great Barrier Reef and Coastal Waters of Queensland*. Angus & Robertson, Sidney, 566 pp.

Munro, I. S. R. 1967. *The Fishes of New Guinea*. Department of Agriculture, Stock and Fisheries, Port Moresby, xxxvii + 650 pp. + 78 plates appended.

Myers, R. F. 1991. *Micronesian Reef Fishes*, Second edition. Coral Graphics, Guam, vi + 298 pp.

Randall, J. E. 1981. *Underwater Guide to Hawaiian Reef Fishes*. Harrowood Books, Newton Square (Pennsylvania), unpaginated.

Randall, J. E. 1982. *A Diver's Guide to Red Sea Reef Fishes*. Immel Publishing, London, unpaginated.

Randall, J. E. 1983a. *Red Sea Reef Fishes*. Immel Publishing, London, 192 pp.

Randall, J. E. 1983b. *Caribbean Reef Fishes*, Second edition. T.F.H. Publications, Neptune City (New Jersey), 350 pp.

Steene, R. C. 1977. *Butterfly and Angelfishes of the World*, Volume 1. John Wiley & Sons, New York, 144 pp. [also see Allen 1979.]

Sterrer, W. (editor). 1986. *Marine Fauna and Flora of Bermuda: A Systematic Guide to the Identification of Marine Organisms*. John Wiley & Sons, New York, xxx + 742 pp.

Stokes, F. J. 1984. *Divers and Snorkelers Guide to the Fishes and Sea Life of the Caribbean, Florida, Bahamas and Bermuda*, Revised edition. Academy of Natural Sciences of Philadelphia, Philadelphia, 160 pp.

Thomson, D. A., L. T. Findley, and A. N. Kerstich. 1979. *Reef Fishes of the Sea of Cortez*. John Wiley & Sons, New York, xv + 302 pp.

Veron, J. E. N. 1986. *Corals of Australia and the Indo-Pacific*. Angus & Robertson, North Ryde (Australia), xi + 644 pp.

Ichthyology, Fish Biology, Invertebrate Zoology, and Marine Botany Texts

Allen, G. R. 1972. *The Anemonefishes: Their Classification and Biology*. T.F.H. Publications, Neptune City (New Jersey), 288 pp.

American Fisheries Society. 1991. *Common and Scientific Names of Fishes from the United States and Canada*, Fifth edition. Special Publication 20, American Fisheries Society, Bethesda (Maryland), 183 pp.

Barnes, R. D. 1987. *Invertebrate Zoology*, Fifth edition. Saunders College Publishing, Philadelphia, ix + 893 pp.

Bold, H. C. and M. J. Wynne. 1978. *Introduction to the Algae: Structure and Reproduction*. Prentice-Hall, Englewood Cliffs (New Jersey), xi + 706 pp.

Bond, C. B. 1979. *Biology of Fishes*. Saunders College Publishing, Philadelphia, vii + 514 pp.

Dawes, C. J. 1981. *Marine Botany*. John Wiley & Sons, New York, x + 628 pp.

Dawson, E. Y. 1966. *Marine Botany: An Introduction*. Holt, Rinehart & Winston, New York, xii + 371 pp.

Lüning, K. 1990. *Seaweeds: Their Environment, Biogeography, and Ecophysiology*. John Wiley & Sons, New York, xii + 527 pp.

Moyle, P. B. and J. J. Cech Jr. 1982. *Fishes: An Introduction to Ichthyology*. Prentice-Hall, Englewood Cliffs (New Jersey), xiv + 593 pp.

Index

Page numbers in *italics* refer to synopses at the beginning of the chapters.